DYSLEXIA IN ADULT EDUCATION: QUESTIONS & ANSWERS

by Denis Lawrence

Dr Denis Lawrence is a chartered educational psychologist and was formerly Chief Educational Psychologist with Somerset County Education Department. He is now in private practice as an educational consultant specialising in the assessment of adults with dyslexia. He is a qualified teacher with experience in primary and secondary schools as well as in universities and colleges of education. This book is based on his research and experience in both Australia and the United Kingdom.

DYSLEXIA IN ADULT EDUCATION
QUESTIONS AND ANSWERS

by DENIS LAWRENCE

The first edition of this book was published in 2007. The second edition, containing the results of the author's research assessing 447 adult students, was published in 2011. This third edition, published in 2012, contains an explanation of the Index scores calculated in the WAIS after assessing adult dyslexic students.

Lulu Publishing

USA

Library of Congress Control Number:

ISBN 978-0-9556762-0-8

Printed and bound by Lulu USA

CONTENTS

ACKNOWLEDGEMENTS

There are many people to thank who have contributed to the publication of this book. Firstly, there are those adult students with dyslexia I have been privileged to meet over the years, too numerous to mention individually, but who have all contributed in their own special way. It has been a humbling experience to meet them and to share their hopes and their fears.

I am indebted to my good friend and former colleague, Dan Williams, who despite his extensive professional commitments, gave up his time to read the manuscript and to make useful suggestions.

A big thank you also to my friends and colleagues in the adult education centres in Cornwall for their sustained encouragement. They are also too numerous to mention them all but space must be found to say thank you to Karen Truscott at HMS Raleigh and to Tamson Waller at the Saltash Link into Learning Centre for their encouraging interest in the book and for supplying useful articles on dyslexia. Thanks also to Stephen Parks at the University College Falmouth for his stimulating discussions on dyslexia.

I would like to pay a special tribute and say thanks to Helen Brauer at the Cornwall Link into Learning service whose enthusiasm for helping those with dyslexia stimulated my own interest in researching the topic. Helen's particular expertise and dedication to assessing and teaching adults with dyslexia has been a continued source of inspiration to me.

Special thanks must go to Patricia Clayton and Helen Irlen for their valuable suggestions and their particular contribution to the section on scotopic sensitivity.

I am most grateful to Mary Anne Kenny for giving up her valuable time to formatting the manuscript and designing the cover. Without her kind and expert help the manuscript would not have reached publication.

Above all, I owe a deep debt of gratitude to my dear wife, Anne, who generously gave her valuable advice and time to read the manuscript, for her advice on computer technology and for her suggestions on amendments to the manuscript. Her support throughout the writing of this book has been invaluable.

Preface

This is an exciting time for adult students with dyslexia as research has led to a clearer understanding of this specific learning difficulty. Over the last decade, there has been a burgeoning of research into both the identification and the treatment of dyslexia. For instance, it had long been observed that dyslexia appeared to run in families (Gilroy and Miles, 1996) but now there is strong evidence for its genetic basis (Raskind & Berninger *et al* 2000). Its neurological origins have also been well established (Berninger and Richards, 2002).

Dyslexia can take many forms and today more sophisticated and more precise methods of identifying dyslexia have been introduced. Also, there are now available reliable screening tests for dyslexia that can be administered by non-specialists in this field.

Methods of assessing dyslexia previously focused on the identification of cognitive weaknesses displayed by those considered dyslexic. However, some evidence is accumulating to indicate that it might be more useful to regard dyslexia not as a deficit after all but rather as a difference in learning style (Mortimore and Tilly, 2004).

The current emphasis on digital technology in education seems to favour visual thinking skills and there is evidence that it is these skills that are often well developed in students with dyslexia. Accordingly, psychological assessments now usually set out to identify possible strengths, as well as identifying possible weaknesses.

The dissemination of the results of the extensive research into dyslexia has resulted in an increase in public awareness of dyslexia. This has culminated in a more optimistic outlook for dyslexic people, particularly those who wish to enter formal education. These new developments in the general field of dyslexia have had a particular impact on staff working with dyslexic students in colleges and universities, providing them with fresh challenges.

In addition to their usual workload, staff are now expected to keep abreast with increasing information resulting from this new research. Also, lecturers are often expected to adjust their teaching methods to accommodate the special needs of dyslexic students. As a result, the educational climate in general today is more supportive of adult students with dyslexia than in previous years. Adult students with dyslexia at all levels of education are receiving increasing support of both a practical and an emotional kind. Formal support for adult students with dyslexia is now offered in most educational institutions. In the past, many students identified as dyslexic when at school were known to avoid further academic studies after school age. In the present educational climate, adult students with dyslexia no longer need feel apprehensive over re-entering education.

Support for students with dyslexia was given particular impetus in the United Kingdom with the *Special Educational Needs & Disability* (SEND) *Act*, 2001. This *Act* empowered all educational institutions to provide services to support students with dyslexia. The recommendations contained in the *Disability Discrimination Act,* 1995 were at last brought into the educational sphere. Among other recommendations, this meant that educational institutions would no longer discourage dyslexic students from studying a particular course on the grounds that they were dyslexic.

The *SEND Act 2001* in the United Kingdom, was admirable in its encouragement to educational institutions to establish support for students with a disability and, today, most educational institutions are doing stalwart work in this area. The majority of educational institutions have purpose-built dyslexia support departments and regularly offer administrative and technical support to students identified as being dyslexic. Many of these establishments ensure regular dissemination of information on dyslexia to their staff as well giving guidance to tutors and lecturers on how best to help dyslexic students on their courses.

Most staff in adult education have been only too willing to accept the new challenges that have emerged as a result of the recent research into dyslexia, but it is clear that many staff would welcome more information on how best to help dyslexic students. However, unless they are specialising in this area of work, it is not always easy for them to become sufficiently informed about the concept of dyslexia and how it can affect their students' performance. They naturally feel concerned about this. In the experience of the author, the professional staff who work in adult education are in need of easy-to-read literature that gives jargon-free information on the topic of dyslexia. As the research and literature on dyslexia is steadily increasing it is becoming even more difficult to keep abreast of developments in this field. Almost invariably, staff lament the fact that it is extremely time-consuming having to wade through voluminous literature in order to obtain the information they seek on the topic. This is an almost impossible task for some of them when teaching their own subject usually kept them fully occupied. It becomes an even more formidable task where learning difficulties is not their particular area of expertise.

One identified major need appears to be for a clearer understanding of exactly what is meant by the term dyslexia. Many professionals express concern over the observation that there seem to be different definitions of dyslexia. Although there is some agreement in the United Kingdom on a working definition of this learning difficulty (British Psychological Society, 1999), it is true that an international consensus of a definition has yet to be achieved. Despite this concern over a definition of dyslexia, there is general agreement on the symptoms manifested by those people known as being dyslexic.

Although many dyslexic students entering adult education were assessed as being dyslexic when at school, there is a large number who are not identified as dyslexic until after beginning their adult studies.

Dyslexia is often discovered for the first time as a result of a college screening programme designed to identify symptoms of dyslexia. Where symptoms of dyslexia are subsequently identified through this screening procedure many of these students then go through a period of anxiety and confusion. To be told for the first time as adults that they have dyslexia can be quite a shock for some. At this time the formal support services for dyslexic students are especially welcome and this is where professional staff need to be aware that these students often need their emotional support. While it is not suggested that all staff receive training in counselling, there are communication skills that they can quickly learn in order to support those students who may require it. One of the aims of this book is to show staff how they might learn these support skills.

After the psychological assessment it would be the normal procedure for a report to be issued. This report usually contains a summary of the test results, together with specific recommendations for supporting the student. Unless special education is their particular area of expertise, most professionals do not always find these reports easy to interpret. A common source of confusion is the statistical language and the statistics used to record the test results. Without some knowledge of statistical theory, test results can be confusing and may even appear to be meaningless. This book aims to help non-specialist staff as well as the dyslexic students, understand these reports and also the statistics used.

A psychological report can generate both positive and negative emotions in students and many students react adversely following the receipt of their psychological report. To be suddenly given a label that is considered to be an official classification of a disability can be uncomfortable and disturbing to a student. The 'disability' label is also often a worry for students when first identified as being dyslexic. It is reassuring to be informed that this label is for administrative purposes only and is not mean to imply that dyslexia is a pathological condition.

Some students have been known to express concern that the confirmed presence of a disability called dyslexia means that they have some kind of 'brain problem'. Again, this highlights the need students often have for an informed and sympathetic person to explain to them what the term dyslexia means. This is when they welcome emotional support as well as accurate information on the meaning of dyslexia. Students are surprised, as well as relieved, when informed that there is no evidence for something being 'wrong with their brain'. They experience further relief on being informed that dyslexia is usually an educational condition and only rarely a medical one.

On the positive side, when assessed as being dyslexic, students are often relieved that they have been given an acceptable reason for their learning difficulties. This is invariably because, prior to the confirmation of their dyslexia, many students had considered their problems to be due to limited ability. To be informed that they are not ‘unintelligent’ can be a tremendous morale booster and an aid to motivation.

It can be appreciated, from the foregoing discussion, that when students are considered to have the specific educational difficulty, known as dyslexia, they are likely to have needs of both an educational and an emotional kind. The professionals who come onto regular contact with dyslexic students need to be aware of these needs.

It is also helpful if staff are aware of the formal support services available in order to redirect a student to those when appropriate. Formal support services are discussed in this book together with the various emotional and practical support mechanisms available to dyslexic students. These are usually recommended in the psychological report following their assessment. As well as for possible formal counseling and perhaps remedial help, there are often many other recommendations in a report.

Examples of these recommendations might be technical equipment such as computers, spellcheckers and dictaphones, as well as extra time in examinations. Professional staff should have this information.

The overall aim of this book therefore is to provide all professionals who come into regular contact with adult students with dyslexia, as well as the students themselves, with useful information on the meaning of dyslexia. The book should also provide reassurance to the many dedicated professionals working with dyslexia students by showing them how best to support students with dyslexia. This applies not only to the teaching staff but also those who have regular contact with the dyslexic students such as psychologists, social workers, counsellors and other health professionals. Student teachers and others on professional training courses who intend to work with adult students with dyslexia should also find this book a useful resource.

Introduction

The first edition of this book was described as being unique in the general field of adult dyslexia as it was based on actual questions posed to the author by adult students referred for investigation of possible dyslexia. These questions had been put to the author mainly by adult students in various educational institutions such as the armed forces, further and higher education and adult education centres. Some of the questions had been posed by tutors, lecturers, psychologists, social workers, counsellors, medical personnel and probation officers. The questions ranged from the practical to the theoretical in nature.

The second and third editions have been written in order to include significant research into dyslexia conducted by the author. The main feature of this research is its analysis of the test results of 447 students who had been referred to the author for assessment of dyslexia. (See *Appendix 6).*

The most commonly asked question by the professionals with dyslexic adult students is, 'What is dyslexia?'. Accordingly, in *Chapter One* the history of the concept of dyslexia is outlined, including the origins of the word dyslexia, together with the current estimation of the numbers of adults with dyslexia in formal education

The multi-faceted nature of dyslexia is then outlined and explored. The common symptoms of dyslexia are listed, showing how dyslexia is often different in each individual. Emphasis is give for the observation that people do not necessarily manifest all of the listed characteristics of dyslexia.

Some people have queried the existence of dyslexia as a valid concept. Accordingly, the first chapter concludes with an account of some significant research findings to provide evidence and reassurance that dyslexia is indeed a valid concept. The conclusions from this research show how dyslexia is considered to be of biological origin even though its treatment may remain educational.

Many people have asked how to distinguish dyslexia from other specific learning difficulties. This question is understandable as there are other common learning difficulties that are related to dyslexia and can overlap dyslexia and are sometimes confused with dyslexia. These learning difficulties are described in *Chapter Two*; they include dyspraxia, dysgraphia, dyscalculia, Irlen syndrome, binocular instability, attention deficit hyperactivity syndrome, autism and Asperger's syndrome. It is advocated in this book that the definitions of these other difficulties be kept separate from a definition of dyslexia.

The topic of whether dyslexia is a difference of learning style rather than a deficit has been raised in the literature. Some recent research into learning styles has hypothesised that people generally tend to favour one sense when learning, over all others. For instance, some may prefer to use vision when attending a lecture while others may prefer to listen to a lecture. There is some evidence that people with dyslexia often favour a visual approach to learning. The current debate over learning styles as a possible alternative explanation of dyslexia is also explored in *Chapter Two.*

How to define dyslexia has been a matter for debate over several years. Practitioners in educational institutions often ask for a definition of dyslexia. They are surprised and frustrated on discovering that to date there is no universally agreed definition of dyslexia. *Chapter Three* begins by discussing the reasons for the difficulty in arriving at a consensus on a definition of dyslexia.

The dyslexia concept has had a chequered history and this is reflected in its varying definitions over the years. This chapter shows how different theoretical perspectives have led to three different kinds of theory that in turn have been responsible for three different kinds of definition of dyslexia.

In the search for an acceptable definition of dyslexia, particular reference is made to a discrepancy between working memory and reasoning ability that has been found to be a common feature of dyslexia. The concept of working memory is explained and discussed in this chapter, with reference to working memory in both the auditory and verbal spheres. This is followed by a summary of the main existing definitions of dyslexia that have been offered over the years.. Each of these is criticised as being unsuitable, in the light of recent research, as a definition that could be applied today. A definition is then offered that draws on the existing definitions and theories as well as supported by the analysis of students' test results conducted by the author and presented in Appendix Six and discussed in *Chapter Three*.. Finally in this chapter, it is advocated that this definition of dyslexia could be universally acceptable for children and adults and would be distinct from other related specific learning difficulties.

Chapter Four answers the question of what tests are available for tutors and lecturers to use to identify dyslexia. Professional staff often ask for information on suitable tests they might use. The chapter begins by outlining the role that professional staff in educational institutions can play in the identification of possible dyslexia in their students. The various screening procedures available for the identification of dyslexia are outlined. These tests range from the completion of checklists of symptoms to self-administered computer programmes. More detailed tests that are usually administered through individual testing by a suitably qualified teacher, psychologist or dyslexia specialist are also described..

The uses and also the limitations of these procedures are presented. It is emphasised that decisions on an individual person should never be made solely on screening procedures. However, they are useful in deciding whether further more specialised detailed testing would be required. If the screening tests reveal a positive result a referral to a psychologist, or to a qualified tester of dyslexia, would need to be arranged before the dyslexia could be confirmed. The importance of explaining this procedure to the student is discussed.

Some professional staff express concern over having to refer a student for a psychological assessment. The question has been raised whether this procedure is always necessary, particularly where a student may be anxious about having a psychological assessment. A common source of this anxiety is that both the staff and the student are not always familiar with the role of a psychologist. Therefore the role of the psychologist or of a specialist assessor in the assessment for dyslexia is clarified in this chapter. Also details of the qualifications and of the psychologist's training are outlined.

Before a referral is made for a detailed psychological assessment many staff quite reasonably need to know exactly what the psychological assessment entails. The question is often asked whether the tests used are different from the tests used by tutors and lecturers. *Chapter Five* answers this question by describing the specialist tests often used by psychologists in their assessment. The chapter begins by explaining why it is necessary to have a measure of intelligence when assessing for dyslexia. As well as the major intelligence tests used other additional cognitive tests that may also be used are briefly described in *Chapter Five.*

The administration of additional tests may sometimes require a further assessment session. Additionally, reference is made to the total length of time generally taken for a detailed psychological assessment. In some instances a psychologist may consider it necessary to administer tests of non-cognitive functions. These tests measure such traits as motivation, anxiety, locus of control and self-esteem. The chapter concludes with a description of these tests and a discussion on their relevance in addition to the cognitive tests.

After the psychological assessment is made it would be the normal procedure for a psychological report to be issued. This report usually contains a summary of the test results, together with specific recommendations for supporting the student. The interpretation of the psychological report is regularly the focus of questions. Unless special education is their particular area of expertise, most professionals and students find these reports difficult to interpret. *Chapter Six* answers the questions commonly asked when interpreting a psychological report.

This chapter acknowledges that the reports often use specialist psychological language as well as formal statistics. Without some knowledge of statistical theory, test results can be confusing and may even appear to be meaningless. An explanation of the basic statistics and the psychological terms used in the psychological report is given. *Chapter Six* concludes with a discussion on the need to record test behaviour that can have an influence on test results.

A major challenge for staff is how best to give practical support to students who are dyslexic. 'How can I best support a student with dyslexia?' is probably the most often asked question after what is the meaning of dyslexia. Staff need information regarding the formal support services available in order to redirect a student to those when appropriate. Formal support services are discussed in *Chapter Seven* together with the practical support mechanisms available to dyslexic students. These are usually recommended in the psychological report following their assessment. Other possible recommendations for practical support are also discussed in this chapter. *Chapter Seven* outlines the general and technical support commonly available to students with dyslexia.

The chapter begins with reference to the legal entitlement for financial support available in the United Kingdom for which most students in higher education with dyslexia can apply. This is followed by an outline of the different types of support that can be provided by tutors or lecturers during their teaching. Support that can be given in examinations and the provision of appropriate study skills assistance is also discussed. *Chapter Seven* concludes with particular study skills strategies that staff might communicate to those students who have expressed a wish to support themselves.

Many tutors and lectures ask why some students demonstrate emotional needs while others seem to cope quite well enough without needing help. *Chapter Eight* answers this question by outlining some significant research into personality development. The research delineating basic structures of personality is outlined showing why it is that people often behave and react emotionally in different ways to the same frustrations. The common ways people have of dealing with frustration are also outlined.

The research into the importance of using the correct words to communicate with people has received some publicity in social psychological research. Many professional staff are aware of this and are also aware that there are techniques available for improving communication skills. Many members of staff have asked for information on these techniques.

A model of communication is outlined in *Chapter Eight* for those professionals who may be interested in improving communication with dyslexic students. This model highlights the principles of non-verbal communication as well as verbal communication. *Chapter Eight* also discusses the three main desirable personal qualities that are shown by the research to be conducive to better communication.

Students with serious emotional issues tend to be referred fairly quickly to appropriate staff such as counsellors, for professional help. The question often posed by tutors and lecturers is how best to respond to those students who do not seem to have serious problems but who do seem to be troubled by their dyslexia. It is not advocated that staff should become counsellors but sometimes they may find themselves in a quasi-counselling role with this kind of student. *Chapter Nine* outlines techniques that professional staff might use in order to support those students.

The chapter begins by describing and explaining the different kinds of emotional needs often presented by dyslexic students. In particular the development of low self-esteem is described and how this affects performance in academic work. The chapter outlines ways in which the tutor or lecturer, through the organisation of a self-esteem enhancing learning environment, can help maintain the student's self-esteem.

The relationship between anxiety and learning is also discussed in *Chapter Nine.* A self-help method of coping with anxiety based on cognitive behavioral therapy is presented. Chapter Nine concludes by outlining how students with dyslexia might be helped to improve their self-esteem through a self-help ten-day programme for use at home.

Chapter 10 discusses life prospects for the student with dyslexia after leaving formal education. Having formed a close relationship with their students many staff are interested to know whether they should prepare students with dyslexia for possible stresses they might face once they have left the relatively sheltered education environment. Society's attitudes towards dyslexia are discussed in this respect. A parallel is drawn between dyslexia that cannot be observed directly and other 'hidden disabilities' such as a hearing problem. Some myths surrounding the concept of dyslexia are discussed.

The problems associated with dyslexia in the work place are raised in this chapter with examples of jobs and careers that are especially suited to those with dyslexia as well as examples of those jobs which they might prefer to avoid.

There is some evidence for dyslexia being inherited and the challenges this presents for parents with dyslexia are discussed in *Chapter Ten.* It can be a particular challenge for them if their children have difficulties with school-work. Not all schools are fully equipped to deal with pupils who are dyslexic.

There are many adults these days in attendance at basic adult education classes. Local authority education departments often organise classes in literacy skills for older adults. It is not uncommon to discover in these classes dyslexic adults who were not identified as being dyslexic when at school. The staff in these particular institutions comprises not only professionals but also many dedicated non-professional volunteers. Both these groups of tutors/lecturers regularly ask for information on dyslexia. Reference is made in this final chapter to the valuable service being offered by these people.

The final section of *Chapter Ten* discusses the difficulties with social relationships often encountered by people with dyslexia. The challenges that these social relationships can produce are outlined and suggestions for coping with them are presented. *Chapter Ten* concludes with a discussion on the disadvantages and advantages of using the label of dyslexia.

It is of interest that many of the questions that that have been personally put to the author that form the basis of this book are among the most relevant issues currently being debated in the research. As knowledge of this complex area accumulates no doubt there will be many more questions to be asked on the topic of adult dyslexia.

Chapter 1
What is dyslexia?

Introduction

The title of this chapter is probably the question most asked, especially by those whose main subject is not in the area of special education. In order to answer this question it is necessary first to trace the history of the concept of dyslexia.

Dyslexia has been a subject of debate in medicine and education for several centuries. Most of this debate has centred on dyslexia as a problem in childhood. It is only in recent times that attention has turned to dyslexia as being an adult problem as well as one for children. A brief history of dyslexia is traced in this chapter beginning with the original interest shown in the problem presented by children

The chapter begins with a discussion of the origins of the word 'dyslexia' and the symptoms of dyslexia before discussing the size of the problem. The chapter continues with a discussion on its beginnings as a medical construct, to the present day view of dyslexia as primarily an educational difficulty. An account of the more recent, significant research into the concept of dyslexia is then presented.

The word dyslexia

The word dyslexia is of Greek origin where 'lexia' refers to language and the prefix 'dys' refers to an absence. Therefore, the word dyslexia refers strictly to an absence of, or a deficit, in the acquisition of language skills.

There is general agreement that the word dyslexia refers to an identifiable group of people that experiences specific learning difficulties in the development of literacy and language skills. It is also agreed that these difficulties often persist in various forms throughout life. However, knowing that a person is labeled as dyslexic does not indicate how best to help that person. The word by itself tells us nothing about the precise problems the person faces, or what to do about them. In order to support a person who is dyslexic we need to know in what areas does the person have difficulties and also how severe is the dyslexia? It is not possible to understand the nature of a person's learning difficulties simply by knowing that they have been diagnosed with dyslexia. The label 'dyslexia' tells us no more than that the person concerned has a specific learning difficulty.

Dyslexia as a multifaceted concept.

Most researchers would accept that dyslexia is a multifaceted concept.. The following list of behaviours would be amongst those that often describe this learning difficulty.

Limited reading attainment

Spelling difficulties

Illegible handwriting and slow to write

Difficulty with recalling information

Slow to respond to orally presented information

Slow to process visual information, e.g.copying from a board

Finds organising the day's tasks difficult

Difficulty recalling phone numbers

Easily forgets verbal instructions

Often confuses left from right and slow to select left & right

Sometimes confuses the order of words when writing and in speaking

Has difficulty with mental arithmetic

Often forgets appointments

Finds map reading difficult

Has difficulty filling in forms

Often mispronounces words in conversation & confuses their order

Sometimes reverses letters and words

It is important to recognise that the above list of behaviours is not exhaustive and also that it would be rare for people with dyslexia to manifest all of the above symptoms at the same time. Difficulties could be experienced in any of the areas listed above and also in various combinations of these symptoms (Galaburda, 1999). Also, many of these symptoms can occur in other kinds of learning difficulties apart from dyslexia. Moreover, there is some disagreement over exactly what combination of these symptoms has to be present before the label dyslexia is given.

It is also important to note that most people at one time or another show some of the symptoms listed above at some stage in their lives. The difference is that in dyslexia symptoms tend to persist and to have possible repercussions on all areas of a person's life. With dyslexic adults their difficulties would be manifested not only in literacy or

learning but also in various aspects of everyday living as described in *Chapter 10*

.

Many of the above behaviours listed can be manifested in both children and adults. Adults with dyslexia however have additional problems in this area that are not necessarily experienced by the dyslexic child. Overall, the problems experienced by the adult with dyslexia are much more complex. This topic is pursued further in *Chapter 10*.

The size of the problem

It is difficult to be precise regarding the number of people in the population with dyslexia. The main reason for this is that the different surveys that have been done tend to vary in their definitions of dyslexia. Surveys have traditionally been organised by presenting to a random population a list of behaviours considered to be symptoms of dyslexia. Unfortunately, this list has often differed according to the particular research interests of the research worker. Consequently, there have been many different estimates of the size of the problem. However, most authorities would agree that between 4% and 10% of the general population has dyslexia, no matter how it is defined. The number of adults with dyslexia in formal education is probably higher than this as many adults were in school before dyslexia was recognised.

A national survey of the numbers of dyslexics in 234 higher education institutions in the United Kingdom was conducted in 1996 (Singleton, 1996). The number of students identified with dyslexia in this survey was found to be 35%. Of some concern is the fact that 43% of these students who are dyslexic were not identified as such until having entered higher education. This suggests at first sight that many schools are poor at identifying children with the problem. Perhaps it is not surprising that schools are not identifying these children as dyslexic when the definition of dyslexia is still unclear. Moreover, it is likely that there are students in further and higher education who are dyslexic but who have never been diagnosed and continue to struggle to achieve without knowing that their difficulties are due to dyslexia.

Early history of the concept of dyslexia

Societal interest in the concept of dyslexia began in 1891 with a report in *The Lancet* medical journal by a Dr. Dejerne. Amongst several other functions, a patient had lost the ability to read, following a brain injury, after having been hit on the head with a crowbar. A medical hypothesis then emerged that concluded that those who had difficulty reading had probably suffered a brain injury. It is of note that these were the days before psychology had come of age. At that time difficulties in learning were considered to in the province of the medical profession. It is only in relatively recent times that

educational psychology has been recognised as having more to contribute to the topic of dyslexia than has the discipline of medicine.

Following the Dejerne's report in *The Lancet*, further accounts began to appear in other medical journals reporting patients who had suffered head injuries and subsequently lost the ability to read. As a result, the view that persistent reading difficulties owed their origins to particular brain dysfunctions began to be generally accepted. The fact that this was merely a hypothesis and not based on any valid research was ignored.

Word blindness

A German neurologist in 1878, Adolph Kussmaul, was probably the first to refer to 'word blindness' as a reason for a literacy difficulty when a patient of his regularly used words in the wrong order. Eventually, in the early 20th century, the term, Word Blindness, appeared in the medical journals for children who had difficulty learning to read. This term owed its origin to the hypothesis that reading difficulties were related to problems with eyesight. It was the view of many in the medical profession of the day that a congenital defect in the brain related to sight was likely to be the cause of reading difficulties. This view was promulgated by the work of a Scottish eye surgeon, Dr James Hinshelwood.

Strephosymbolia

A further development of some significance occurred in the early history of the concept of dyslexia. In 1925, Dr Orton, an American neurologist, introduced another term called 'strephosymbolia', for children who tended to reverse letters. He also introduced a second term called 'developmental alexia' to describe children with reading difficulties. However, these terms were only short-lived in the literature. Before long, the concept of dyslexia came into more general usage. Thereafter dyslexia was defined as a medical diagnosis describing an identifiable group of children who had learning difficulties that were manifested mainly in the broad sphere of the acquisition of literacy skills.

In those early days of the history of the concept, dyslexia was considered to be an inherited condition found in some children. This was thought to be true even though at that time there was no empirical evidence to support this view. The possibility that dyslexia might continue into adulthood was not even considered at this time. Moreover, consistent with the medical model of behaviour that dominated this period, dyslexia was considered to be a pathological condition.

Dyslexia as a medical problem

It may seem odd in the light of the voluminous educational and psychological research into dyslexia being conducted today that in the nineteenth and early 20th century the topic of children with literacy

difficulties was considered to be a medical problem. However, perhaps this is not so surprising considering that in those days mainstream psychology was still wrestling with the problem of introspection as a method of psychological investigation and was struggling to establish itself as a science in its own right. Consequently, psychology had little to offer on the debate on the identification and treatment of learning difficulties. Educational psychology, as a specific branch of applied psychology, had not yet emerged.

Throughout this early history of the concept, neither psychology nor the teaching profession made any significant contribution to the debate on dyslexia. Many educationalists were sceptical and it was not uncommon for the view to be expressed by some teachers that there was no such thing as dyslexia. This opinion was understandable when there was still no valid research available on the topic. At that time, children who had literacy difficulties were considered to be either constitutionally slow or poorly motivated toward learning.

Just how this particular view could hold prominence is hard to appreciate today in the light of our increased knowledge regarding how children learn. Again, this is not so surprising considering that in the 19th and early 20th century educational research journals were few in number so that even if scientific studies had taken place there was no reputable avenue for the promulgation of results.

Despite the continued interest shown by the medical profession into the topic of children's learning difficulties the medical profession did not appear to have any real practical advice for the teacher in the classroom. No matter what were the origins of the problem, these children still had to be taught. Neurological theories had little to offer in that direction until 1925 when the exception that proved the rule appeared with the publication of recommended teaching procedures written by the neurologist, Dr Orton, referred to in the previous section. He was later to collaborate with Anna Gillingham and Bessie Stillman (1936), educationalists, in the publication of the first teaching method based on an analysis of language for children who had reading difficulties. This was a multi-sensory approach based on the structure of language and was an innovation in its day. This publication led to an interest in how all children learn to read and was the forerunner of research into the phonological aspects of reading.

Dyslexia continued to be researched as deficits until Galaburda (1984) who asserted that dyslexia is a normal variation of the development of the brain and is not a disorder. He found abnormalities in the left brain of dyslexics on whom he had performed autopsies but in so doing he noticed also that there was a superior development of the right hemisphere in dyslexics. This has since given rise to the view amongst some authors that dyslexia may not be a deficit of functioning after all but instead it may be simply a difference of functioning.

Today, the existence of dyslexia has been empirically demonstrated and conclusions from some of the more significant current research findings are summarised below.

Recent significant research findings

Phonological processing

Phonological processing refers to the ability to associate sounds with letters and also to be able to break down words into their sounds. Most researchers would agree that phonological processing ability is the basic skill in being able to read successfully (Snowling, 1995).

Deficits on phonological processing have received prominent attention in the research.

It is generally acknowledged that many instances of reading difficulty reflect deficits in phonological processing in both children and adults (Fawcett and Nicolson, 2001). They will have difficulty sounding out new words and also be slow to decode them. Fawcett and Nicholson describe these people as lacking in 'automaticity'. Some authors would claim that a delay in phonological processing ability in young children is a valid predictor of future dyslexia (Hagvet, 1997).

There is evidence that dyslexic people often have a difficulty with retaining phonological information and also with attaching verbal labels to visual information (Pickering, 2001). Fawcett and Nicolson have shown how dyslexics have difficulty with visual processing and how this is likely to be related to gross motor skills.

Deficits in working memory

Most researchers would agree that a weakness in working memory is associated with dyslexia. (Nicolson, Fawcett and Baddeley, 1992). Moreover, there is some evidence that there is a link between the language area of the brain and the part that is associated with memory function (Gathercole and Baddeley, 1993). Research has shown that that those with dyslexia rely more on semantics, the meanings of words, and less on the analysis of words. This is fine with words that have already been learned and are regularly used but with new words the person with dyslexia will always have a problem.

This research into the part played by working memory has reawakened interest in possible underlying neurological causes of dyslexia (Pavlidis, 1990). Further support for the role of working memory in dyslexia has come from neurological research using magnetic resonance imaging.

The importance of assessing working memory when considering dyslexia was given further significance in an analysis by the author of 447 students in adult education. (Lawrence, 2009). Deficits in working memory in relation to non-verbal intelligence were discovered in 97% of the population. The deficit between working memory and verbal intelligence was 95%.

Neurological factors

As described above, dyslexia research in the early 20th century was conducted mainly through clinical studies of individuals with brain injuries where they had lost abilities in specific areas of the brain. Today, in the 21st century, the study of brain functioning has become more refined, and also more reliable, through the use of a technique known as functional Magnetic Resonance Imaging (fMRI). Using this technique it is possible now, by measuring the blood flow, to pinpoint areas of the brain that are being activated at any given moment. This technique has given further support to the early discoveries when treating brain injured people that the different hemispheres are activated differently with different tasks (Springer and Deutch, 1998). It is probably true to say that the fMRI technique has revolutionised neurological research and is continuing to do so.

In some studies of that part of the brain known as the temporal lobe it was found that there was an unusual balance between the lobes in people diagnosed as having dyslexia (Frith, 1996). Using the fMRI technique it seems from these studies that the temporal lobe in non-dyslexic people shows asymmetry, whereas those with dyslexia shows either symmetry or the right side is greater than the left side. The full significance of this finding is yet to be understood.

Research into dyslexia using the fMRI technique has provided further support for the association between dyslexia and weaknesses in phonological processing. The ability to read is dependent primarily on being able to detect phonemes (associating letters with sounds) and to be able to combine them into words. There is ample research demonstrating that those who have difficulty learning to read usually have a problem with phonemes. As referred to earlier, phonic analysis ability is known to be a basic skill in learning to read successfully. Through the fMRI technique it has been seen that the area concerned with analysing the phonemes is not as well activated in those with dyslexia as it is in the case of normal readers.

An important conclusion from using the fMRI technique to investigate the language centres is that the areas of the brain concerned with recognising and analysing phonemes are linked even more strongly to the brain's memory processes than they are to the language centres. It seems that people with dyslexia concentrate more on trying to remember words than they do on trying to understand them. It is likely therefore that a weakness in working memory is a major problem faced by adults with dyslexia, causing them to be slow to process information. This apparent weakness in working memory forms the essence of a new definition of dyslexia offered in the next chapter.

Although in practice the brain is seen to work as a whole entity, research into brain functioning has revealed that the two hemispheres operate with a different emphasis with regard to different tasks (Springer and Deutsch, 1998). It has long been known that the left side of the brain is more involved than the right side of the brain in the development of general language skills (Shaywitz, 1996). More specifically, research into reading acquisition has also identified the left side of the brain as being activated more than the right side in the process of acquiring the skill of reading and also with logical thought. In contrast, the right side of the brain is seen to be more involved with analysing visuo-spatial information and to be more involved in creative thinking (Geschwind and Galaburda, 1985). At the risk of oversimplifying the results of this kind of research it would seem to indicate that the people diagnosed as dyslexic are probably using their right brain more than their left-brain. In other words, they have developed their creativity and facility for visuo-spatial relationship which is centred on the right brain, more than their language skills, centred on the left brain. Although there is evidence for greater left hemisphere involvement in language processing, there is also some evidence to show that the right hemisphere of the brain also has a part to play in language facility (Luria, 1974). It has been suggested that the right hemisphere of the brain is better at comprehending words than the left (Springer and Deutsch, 1998).

Given that people with dyslexia appear to have difficulty with left-brain activity, it would not be unreasonable to hypothesise that they are more at ease with right brain activity. If this were the case it should mean that people with dyslexia would be more likely to choose practical subjects for study that depend mainly on the visuo-spatial

areas of the brain. It would follow then art and art related courses in higher and further education would contain a greater number of people with dyslexia. Anecdotal evidence would suggest that this is indeed the case.

Laterality

Laterality refers to the development of lateral dominance. Most people eventually establish dominance of eye, hand and leg so have a tendency to use either their left side or their right side according to which hemisphere in the brain has developed dominance (Harris, 1979). Sometimes however, there is a delay in the development of dominance and in some cases dominance is never properly established. A common symptom of young children is a tendency to reverse letters such as "b" and "d". When there is a delay in developing dominance this is referred to as lateral confusion. While in children with dyslexia this is not uncommon, adults have usually learned how to overcome this problem with years of practice. However, the need to reverse things sometimes persists into adulthood. In the research conducted by the author (Lawrence, 2009) 60.4% of the sample had confused laterality but 95% had lateral confusion combined with scotopic sensitivity. It is evident that scotopic sensitivity should form part of any assessment for dyslexia. Again, in the Lawrence research 95.5% of dyslexic students had below average processing speed. It is not possible of course to determine whether this was due to lateral confusion or scotopic sensitivity, or due to a combination of factors.

Although adults will usually have learned over time which is left and which is right, there is often a slight delay when having to choose left from right. It has been suggested that this tendency to reversals is a function of the asymmetry of the brain (Herbert M.R. *et al* (2004).

An interesting area of research is the relationship between left-handed people, dyslexia and speech. Although the research evidence in this area is far from conclusive there is evidence of a higher proportion of dyslexia in left-handed people (Geschwind & Behan

1982). Furthermore, there is some evidence that speech, in about one third of left-handed people, is located either in the right hemisphere or in both hemispheres. This is in contrast to right-handed people where language is located in the right hemisphere.

In the Lawrence research referred to above amongst 447 adult dyslexic students, 60% of the population were discovered to have lateral confusion.

Magno-cellular systems

Magnocells are large neurones in the brain that control sensory and motor events. It has also been suggested that magnocells in the brain also control both the timing of visual and motor events. If this is indeed shown to be the case then a deficit in magnocells could mean that there would be problems with the synchronisation of events such as visual tracking while reading. Eye movements would not be synchronised with the perceived visual input. This would cause slowness to read as well as a tendency to confuse the order of words and letters.

It has been suggested that there may be magnocells also in the auditory sphere resulting in a weakness in auditory sequential memory. If these possibilities eventually were shown to be the case then this would be further evidence for the neurological origins of dyslexia.

Research into the visual magno-cellular system in the brain suggests the possibility that these large neurons may be deficient in those with dyslexia (Borsting, 1996). As the magno-cells, situated in the mid-brain, are responsible for the timing of sensory events and their coordination with visual and auditory events, a weakness here might lead to the confusion of the order of letters and words when writing and reading. This might account also for the slowness of dyslexics to process both visual and auditory information. Demb, *et al* (1988) have shown how dyslexic children in their study had abnormalities of the magno-cellular systems of the visual cortex. Research confirming the same problem with adults is continuing.

Cerebellar weaknesses

The cerebellum in the brain has traditionally been found to be involved mainly in movement and balance. However, there is evidence that the cerebellum is also involved in the acquisition of language. It is perhaps not surprising therefore to discover that there is a link between impairment of the cerebellum and dyslexia (Nicolson and Fawcett, 1997). Some recent research in the University of Texas has given further support for this view and also has suggested that, in addition, the cerebellum monitors incoming sensory information (Parsons *et al* 2000). If this can be shown to be the case, then an abnormal cerebellum could well be the main reason for spelling and reading difficulties. Recent research into the role played by the cerebellum has led to the further development of exercise-based programmmes such as the Dore Programme (Dore, 2006). There are several university research centres investigating the claims for this particular remedial programme to be a 'miracle cure' for dyslexia.

Genetics

It has always been suspected that dyslexia was inherited and now there is evidence that dyslexia is mainly an inherited condition (Fagenheim, 1999). Research has identified genes on chromosome six and chromosome 15 as being mainly responsible for dyslexia, with genes on chromosomes one and fifteen also playing a part (Fisher and Smith, 2001). This is not to deny that environmental factors also play a part. For instance, dyslexia in some people can occur as the result of a head injury. In this case, the difficulty would be referred to as secondary dyslexia or acquired dyslexia.

Conclusions .

There is little doubt that the research into the possible origins of dyslexia has contributed immensely to our understanding of this

specific learning difficulty and also to the management of the problem. Deficits in working memory, confused laterality and slowness to process information are clearly outward signs of dyslexia. Deficits in phonological analysis ability are also commonly seen. Despite the fascinating research, the treatment of this specific learning difficulty has to continue to be educational. Even with the sometimes startling developments in brain research and genetics, it is highly improbable that dyslexia will ever become a subject for treatment by the neurologist or the geneticist. Whatever the origins of the problem it will be in the educational sphere that dyslexia will continue to be treated. While the teaching of dyslexic students should allow for, and often compensate for their observed perceptual difficulties, it would seem that more research into the best methods of teaching dyslexic people is going to be the most useful area for future research.

Summary

The chapter began with a discussion on the meaning of dyslexia and the size of the problem. This was followed by a list of behaviours commonly associated with dyslexia that illustrated its multifaceted nature. The point was made that the variety and degree of symptoms that are referred to as dyslexia have made it difficult to define dyslexia precisely. A brief review of the early historical development of the use of the term dyslexia followed.

Although research into dyslexia began in the medical sphere, it appears to have come full circle as evidenced by the recent research increasingly focusing on the neurology of the brain. This chapter outlined some of the earlier research into the topic that began in the 19th century with a medical model of dyslexia. Over the following years there was a gradual move away from the medical model to an educational one. Much of today's research into the origins of dyslexia appears to be moving once again back towards a medical model of dyslexia, with particular reference to neurological factors. However, despite the remarkable advances in neurological research it is asserted that the treatment of dyslexia will almost certainly continue to be within the educational sphere rather then becoming a subject for neurology.

Chapter 2
How can I distinguish dyslexia from other specific learning difficulties?

Introduction

Dyslexia can sometimes be confused with other types of specific learning difficulties as there are other learning difficulties that can have similar symptoms. It is not surprising therefore if occasionally a staff member queries a diagnosis of dyslexia. This is more likely to happen where the staff member also has knowledge of other specific learning difficulties. These other specific learning difficulties are defined and described in this chapter.

The chapter begins by distinguishing between a general learning difficulty and a specific learning difficulty before going on to outline other specific learning difficulties.

General and specific learning difficulties

Some of the learning difficulties that can so easily be confused with dyslexia are general across all abilities. There are others that are specific learning difficulties, like dyslexia, that are usually restricted to one area of learning

Whereas a general learning difficulty is manifested by difficulties in most areas of intellectual functioning, the test profile of results in the case of a specific learning difficulty would be characterised by a wide variety of test scores. Some scores may be above average and others below average and specific to a particular area. There is agreement that dyslexia is one of these specific learning difficulties. Some authorities have in the past regarded dyslexia as synonymous with the term specific learning difficulty (Rutter and Yule, 1975). Today the term dyslexia is generally regarded as only one of several specific learning difficulties.

The learning difficulties that are related to dyslexia can be grouped under the three headings of cognitive difficulties, sensory difficulties and physical difficulties. It is important to note that although these other learning difficulties can be categorised in this way, the categories are not totally exclusive. Many of these conditions can overlap one another and also may sometimes overlap dyslexia. This is a further argument for defining them precisely and separately from dyslexia and from each other.

Cognitive difficulties

Dyscalculia as part of dyslexia

Dyscalculia is a term that is used to describe a condition whereby people have difficulties with mathematics. There is some evidence that this kind of difficulty may be inherited (Shalev, *et al*, 2001). This difficulty may or may not be part of dyslexia.

It can be appreciated why dyscalculia often accompanies dyslexia if we consider the functions required to be able to do mathematics.

Many of these functions are the same as those involved in the development of literacy skills (Miles and Miles, 1992). For instance, both learning to read and learning how to do mathematics depend on working memory and the ability to process information. This applies whether the information is presented orally or in written form. To be able to perform both these skills it is essential first to be able to hold symbols in short- term memory. It is then necessary to be able process the information, or in other words to be able to make the information meaningful. The information then needs to be expressed either in written form or orally. This is most easily illustrated when attempting to solve a mental arithmetic problem (Chinn and Ashcroft, 1997).

A weakness in auditory sequential memory would be a handicap to successfully completing mental arithmetic problems. This is why one of the tests used in the assessment of dyslexia, described in Chapter 5, comprises a series of mental arithmetic problems. The information has not only to be retained but also to be processed. This ability is similar to that required in taking down notes in a lecture.

A further illustration of dyscalculia accompanying dyslexia would be working with equations in algebra. Again, a weakness in visual sequential memory would be a handicap. Algebra requires the ability to hold in the short-term memory a series of numbers and symbols while at the same time considering a second series of numbers. This would be would be even more difficult if the person concerned also had lateral confusion. A basic skill in the solving of mathematical equations is being able separate left from right (Henderson, 2000).

The initial learning of multiplication tables is a further example of how a person with dyslexia is likely to have difficulties also with mathematics. Both are dependent on short–term memory. Once learned however, information will be stored in long-term memory. People with dyslexia rarely have a weakness in long -term memory.

People with dyslexia who have a weakness in visuo-spatial awareness are likely to have difficulty with the geometry side of mathematics. Again, this subject is particularly difficult for those with lateral confusion and/or a weak visual memory.

Although a common characteristic of dyslexia is a weakness in working memory, dyscalculia is not always present in a person who has been diagnosed as dyslexic.

The reasons for this apparent anomaly are not altogether clear but it seems that some people do have an isolated skill in mathematics despite weaknesses in other areas of intellectual functioning.

Dyscalculia without dyslexia

Not all those who have a problem with mathematics will have dyslexia. Some people have a good working memory, are at least of average intelligence, have strong language skills, but still cannot easily understand the necessary concepts involved in mathematics (Kosc, 1974). These people find it difficult to appreciate how numbers relate to one another. It seems also that they have a problem with the conception of size. They can usually learn the basic mathematical processes and arrive at the correct answers to simple mathematical problems, but they often do so without really understanding the processes. While people with dyscalculia usually have no problem with day-to-day mathematics, as when shopping, they are not able to extend their mathematical abilities beyond the basic skills. The reasons for this are unclear but it is significant that the problem appears to be unrelated to levels of intelligence. Research is currently investigating the origins of this difficulty.

There is another group that manifests difficulties with mathematics but who have neither dyscalculia nor dyslexia. A detailed investigation of their problem often reveals that they have simply missed learning the basic mathematical processes when at school. As a result they have come to believe, probably wrongly, that they would never be able to complete mathematical problems. With appropriate teaching together, with confidence building, this group usually makes good progress.

Attention Deficit Hyperactivity Disorder (ADHD)

There is another condition often confused with dyslexia that is known as Attention Deficit Hyperactivity Syndrome (ADHD). This condition usually results in problems of personality and behaviour as its major feature is a problem with prolonged concentration accompanied by hyperactive motor activity. It can easily be confused with dyslexia as many of the symptoms of ADHD are similar to those manifested by dyslexia. As with dyslexia, a common characteristic of ADHD is a short attention span accompanied by an apparent weakness in short-term memory. The syndrome is more commonly associated with children but some continue to show this type of behaviour even when they become adults. In general, however, by the time these children become adults most of them have usually learned methods of controlling their behaviour.

There appear to be two very different views of the origins of ADHD itself. Whilst most professionals would recognise that there is an identifiable group of people who demonstrate the symptoms known as ADHD, explanations for it are different. Moreover, the explanations tend to lie at different ends of a spectrum. There are those at one end of the spectrum who assert that this is a medical condition requiring medication. At the other end of the spectrum, there are those who assert that ADHD is a non-medical condition to be managed through behavioural methods.

While the arguments continue (Goodman and Poillion, 1992), what is beyond doubt is that those with ADHD and those with dyslexia have many symptoms in common although the reasons for their difficulties may be different. Both are usually slow to develop literacy skills but while the main reason for this in the dyslexic person is usually slowness to develop phonological skills, the main reason in those with ADHD is that they find concentration a problem.

Unless identified early in childhood and treated appropriately people who have the condition known as ADHD will eventually experience frustrations of the same kind as those experienced by people with dyslexia. Both group are prone to demonstrate hyperactive behaviour if their problems are not identified and treated early. Clearly they each require different treatment methods. (See Appendix 3 for screening Check List for ADHD).

Learning styles

Some authors question whether dyslexia might be a particular type of learning style rather than being a cognitive deficit. This view sees dyslexia as a difference of brain functioning rather than a weakness. The topic of learning styles has been well researched over the years in the general area of learning but there has recently been a renewed interest in learning styles with the rising awareness of dyslexia (Cranton, 1992).

A learning style is a term used to describe a consistent and habitual way of learning or organising and processing information. This can be through a preferred sensory mode or through a particular approach of cognitive awareness. Learning styles may overlap and the range of identified learning styles is considerable. It is usually hypothesised that most people have a preferred, or dominant, learning style.

The topic of learning styles in psychology probably began originally with the work of Carl Jung (1923) and has occupied research workers for many years since then. Jung viewed the human personality as functioning in the four modes of sensation, intuition, feeling and thinking. He went on to suggest that one of these functions was dominant in people. The process of maturing for Jung consisted of the eventual development of all these functions to produce a well-rounded personality.

Further research into learning styles was stimulated by the original work of Jung. Although Jung's theories were based on the adult, this original work stimulated others to engage in research into the learning styles of children (Bruner, Goodnow and Austin, 1960). Today, there is research also into how adults learn and empirical evidence to support the view there are basic differences in the way in which adults learn as well as children (Cranton, 1992).

When learning, we take in information from all the five senses – sight, sound, touch, hearing and smell. The hypothesis is that people vary in the emphasis they gave to different senses. For example, some people tend to use sight more than sound so learn more efficiently through visual information. There are others whose preferred mode of learning is auditory so they learn more efficiently listening to a lecture and then discussing it with others. As the research grew it became clear that a multi-sensory approach to teaching was more efficient, especially for those with dyslexia (Mortimore, 2003).

The interest in how people learn resulted in the discovery of other kinds of learning styles, including the original personality patterns suggested by Jung. In problem solving, it seems that some people take a reflective view of the information and think about solutions whereas others might prefer to adopt a more 'hands–on' practical approach to the problem. Again, some people learn best through taking a global approach when tackling a new problem while others seemed to prefer to work in stages tackling one part at a time. Some children preferred to focus on one part of a problem while others preferred to scan the whole. The terms 'focusers' and 'scanners' were introduced to describe people with these different learning styles (Bruner, 1966).

The more recent renewed interest in learning styles has tended to shift the focus away from dyslexia as a disability. The possibility that those with dyslexia might well be demonstrating a difference in learning style has stimulated research into teaching people through their preferred learning style rather than focusing on helping them overcome any weaknesses (Gardiner, 1993).

The current interest in learning styles has led some adult education colleges to use screening programmes designed to identify the preferred learning style of adults. Those with a more visual learning style are considered more likely to be those who subsequently are proved to be dyslexic in accordance with the theory that they tend to use their right brain more than their left brain. There are some authors who would assert that modern living with more emphasis on visual stimulation, such as televisions and computers, is responsible for producing more people with a visual learning style. If this can be shown to be the case then there would be more people in society today who are dyslexic.

The notion that dyslexia is not a deficit but merely a difference is an attractive one. However, while research may eventually demonstrate a positive correlation between learning styles and dyslexia at the time of writing, this correlation has not yet been satisfactorily demonstrated.

Autism and Asperger's Syndrome

As with ADHD these conditions are usually characterised by personality and behavioural problems. In these cases, however, it is mainly the person's difficulties with communication that can sometimes be confused with dyslexia. The main difference between these two syndromes is that people with Asperger's syndrome usually have well developed language skills while those with autism usually have a language difficulty. Both these syndromes range along a continuum from being mild to severe.

People with both of these syndromes appear to be aloof and unable to empathise with other people or to interpret other people's feelings. For example, they tend to react literally to instructions so are unable to appreciate absurdities in another person's speech. As children they were likely to have played unimaginatively. They are particularly lacking in the ability to pick up nonverbal cues so will tend to behave in a socially inept fashion. In the same way as they are unable to appreciate that other people have feelings, they themselves appear to be unable to express emotions. These syndromes are often accompanied by fine and gross motor coordination difficulties. As well as sometimes being confused with dyslexia, these symptoms can also be confused with dyspraxia and ADHD as described above.

There can be a genuine overlap between dyslexia and these syndromes. For instance, people with Asperger's and also those with autism tend to have difficulty making academic progress despite sometimes having a high level of intelligence. They will work at their own pace and often be oblivious of time demands. Accordingly, as those with dyslexia, they will show frustration if demands are made on them to complete a task in an allotted time. Many people with this syndrome lack motivation to perform, so they often lack concentration and give up easily on academic tasks.

It can be appreciated how easy it is to confuse the person with autism or Asperger's syndrome with the person who has dyslexia when so many of their symptoms may be similar. The situation is made more difficult by the fact that they are likely to produce a false positive result on a screening test for dyslexia. This is why once again it is only through a detailed psychological assessment that the condition can be identified as seen to be a personality problem rather than a cognitive difficulty.

Sensory difficulties.

Irlen Syndrome or Scotopic SensitivityThere is an identifiable group of people who have a problem with the physical effort of reading but who in other circumstances have normal vision. They may experience a variety of problems when reading, such as distortions of print, apparent movement of print, problems with visual tracking and unusual glare. Their reading is sometimes characterised by having to place their finger beneath each line to prevent them from losing their place on the paper. This problem is said to originate from sensitivity to particular light frequencies and is not related to visual refractive errors. Although people with this condition are able to read and write, the effort that they put into these activities eventually can result in serious fatigue, slowing down performance.

The term Scotopic Sensitivity Syndrome or-Irlen Sydrome, is used to describe people who have this condition.

Perceptual distortions, experienced by some children, were first noted by Olive Meares, a teacher in New Zealand. She noticed that some of the children she taught seemed to have a problem with glare, causing print distortions, when they were reading.

Helen Irlen in the USA, while researching adults with reading difficulties, also noted perceptual problems, and was the first to catagorise the vast array of perceptual distortions that can occur. Irlen then went on to devise a method for testing and helping individuals with this problem, using coloured overlays and tinted spectacles (Irlen, 1991). She originally named the problem Scotopic Sensitivity Syndrome. After spending the first five years exclusively researching the method with adults, research was expanded to include both children and adults.

In the past, the successful treatment for the Irlen Syndrome was questioned as being a result of the placebo effect, in adults as well as in children. That is, any different treatment will produce a temporary improvement simply by virtue of its novelty. However, long term studies and a strong body of evidence would substantiate the benefits of using Irlen coloured lenses or coloured overlays. There are many sufferers with this condition who claim relief as well as increased speed of reading, improved comprehension, ability to read longer and with less strain upon using coloured lenses or coloured overlays. There are now over 60 research studies documenting change in reading rate, accuracy, comfort and comprehension following the prescription of coloured lenses (Evans, 2001).

The prescription of the filters and also the prescription of coloured lenses became a major commercial venture for many early researchers into this syndrome. The Irlen Institute in California is known worldwide not only for its commercial ventures but also for the spread of Irlen Centres in most parts of the English-speaking world. They are not only involved in assessing for the syndrome but also for conducting valuable research into it. They have also instituted a training programme for future assessors of the condition.

Current research is investigating the use of coloured filters placed over a computer screen to help those with Irlen Syndrome. Additionally, there are research workers in England currently investigating the use of computer programmes that can identify the colour best suited to the individual concerned. Perhaps the most notable is Arnold Wilkins at the University of Cambridge.

The performance of a person during the psychologist's assessment for dyslexia may raise the possibility of scotopic sensitivity. They may, for instance, screw up their eyes when reading or show visual discomfort when having to complete visual tasks and may complain that their eyes are tired and need resting. However, without a skilled assessment from a trained practitioner it would not be possible to positively identify Irlen Syndrome. Most educational psychologists will not be trained in this area of work. It would be necessary, therefore, for those with suspected scotopic sensitivity to seek an assessment from a purpose-trained assessor. There are also several questionnaires available for the purpose of screening for possible scotopic sensitivity. One of these questionnaires is presented in Appendix 5 as an illustration.

Finally in this section, it would seem from the research evidence that there is a distinct group of people with this syndrome. In the Lawrence (2009) study 95% of the sample referred for assessment as probably dyslexic were seen also to have visual discomfort. On the other hand 34% of the same sample has visual discomfort but who otherwise were not showing symptoms of dyslexia.

.Binocular instability

Some people appear to have eye movements when reading that tend to want to go from right to left. This will produce obvious problems when reading as reading for comprehension requires eye movements in the opposite direction. People with this problem are slower than most to read and, in addition, find that they cannot easily fixate on words and letters (Garzia, 1993). The problem is often further exacerbated by the fact that many dyslexics have lateral confusion and have a natural tendency to reverse letters and words. However, while binocular instability slows down the reading process it is difficult to regard this difficulty as an aspect of dyslexia as defined. Research into this interesting area is continuing.

It has also been suggested that a deficit in the magno-cells in the brain that control both the timing of visual and motor events could cause a problem with the synchronisation of events such as visual tracking while reading. In a study by Borsting (1996), 75% of poor readers had defects in the magno-cellular pathways in of the mid brain. A defect in this region of the brain would result in visual information being slowed down en route to the cortex. Eye movements would not be synchronised with the perceived visual input. This may be one explanation why dyslexic students are often slow to read as well as having a tendency to confuse the order of words and letters.

Physical difficulties

Dyspraxia & dysgraphia

Dyspraxia is a term sometimes used to describe people who have a motor coordination weakness. In children, it used to be known as the 'clumsy child syndrome'. Coordination problems in acts such as balancing, walking, kicking a ball and catching a ball are common symptoms of this problem. It seems from the research that there is an association between physical coordination and language skills

(Nicholson, *et al*, 1999). It is known that the cerebellum controls movement and there is also evidence of a link between the cerebellum and the language area of the brain. Deficits in the cerebellum region of the brain have also been seen to cause difficulties with the pronunciation of certain words (Kirby and Drews, 2003).

Although difficulties in gross motor coordination amongst those diagnosed as being dyslexic are not uncommon, by no means all those identified as being dyslexic have motor coordination problems. Conversely, those who show motor coordination problems do not always show learning difficulties.

Fine motor coordination problems are also not uncommonly found in dyslexics. Their handwriting is often illegible and the term dysgraphia is used to define this difficulty. It is significant however that people with these problems do not necessarily show learning difficulties.

In view of the link between the cerebellum and motor coordination, some research workers (Thach, 1996) have developed physical programmes and exercises to improve motor coordination, claiming that this in turn has an effect on literacy skills. The hypothesis is that the various exercises and activities in these programmes integrate other brain functions, including the language areas of the brain. The exercises involve activities such as balancing on a beam and throwing a ball from one hand to the next. This method of treatment gained popularity in the 70's with the development of Paul Dennison's Brain Gym programme for children. Included in Brain Gym programme are various activities designed to develop visual and auditory discrimination as well as physical abilities. The approach is based firmly on the hypothesis that there is an association between these abilities, language development and academic achievement. While there is some research evidence with children showing some benefits from this approach, little work has been done with adults showing its effectiveness.

Summary

The various type of learning difficulty related to dyslexia were discussed in this chapter. They were seen to fall into the categories of cognitive weaknesses, sensory or physical problems and those related to problems of personality.

Each of these other learning difficulties can manifest similar symptoms as dyslexia. It was shown in this chapter how these associated learning difficulties often accompany dyslexia and sometimes overlap it. In the interests of clarity of definition of dyslexia, it was suggested that these other learning difficulties need to be identified as separate from dyslexia. Without a psychological assessment to obtain a differential diagnosis these other learning difficulties can easily mask dyslexia and prevent appropriate treatment.

The debate remains on how best to define dyslexia. A complication in arriving at an acceptable definition of dyslexia would need to recognise the differences in symptoms between the manifestation of the problem in children and adults. This difference and a suggested definition are discussed in the next chapter.

Chapter 3 How Should we define dyslexia?

Introduction

There have been many different definitions and theories of dyslexia over the years and none has been universally accepted. The question of how to define dyslexia has been a matter of controversy and debate amongst professionals working in the field of special education for well over a century and this continues.

The chapter begins by discussing the reasons why it has been difficult to obtain a consensus on a definition of dyslexia. The chapter goes on to show how different theories of dyslexia have been largely responsible for the problem. It discusses how the different definitions that have been postulated over the years can be grouped into the two main categories of causal and descriptive definitions. Examples of these current definitions generated by committees and individual professionals are outlined and a critique of each is presented. It can be seen how different research perspectives have been reflected in the various definitions of dyslexia.

In the search for an acceptable definition of dyslexia, an argument is presented in this chapter for the inclusion of a specific weakness in working memory to be the basis of a definition. In support of this proposal, reference is made to the analysis of the results of a survey conducted by the author gives evidence of a specific weakness in working memory. It is advocated that a universally acceptable definition would also need to incorporate causal, descriptive and discrepancy theoretical perspectives.

One of the reasons why it has not been easy to arrive at a consensus over a definition has been that other related conditions have been found often to accompany, and often to overlap as described in Chapter 2.

The problems in arriving at a definition

There appear to be three main reasons for the difficulty in arriving at a consensus over a definition of dyslexia. The first reason is that attempts to define dyslexia have been unrealistically too all embracing. Dyslexia is a multi-faceted concept as described in Chapter 1. Attempting to affix one label to so many different symptoms has tended to create a misapprehension that dyslexia can be regarded as a single entity. Dyslexia is not something that people have or do not have, as in a medical condition such as measles or mumps. Dyslexia is not a single entity but is a word used to describe a variety of learning difficulties that can be manifested in a variety of different ways.

A second reason for the difficulty in arriving at a consensus has been the difficulty of devising a definition that would accurately define dyslexia in both children and adults. There has been a tendency to assume that manifestations of dyslexia are similar in both children and adults when in fact there are many differences. The ways in which dyslexia is manifested in an adult compared with the ways in which it is manifested in the child are much more complex as well as often very different. The adult may well show many of the same problems as the dyslexic child but the dyslexic adult's problems with dyslexia are usually more complex. The adult with dyslexia has other problems in this area that are not necessarily experienced by the dyslexic child. For instance, unlike the dyslexic child, many dyslexic adults have learned to read although they may continue to have problems with spelling. The different challenges faced by the adult with dyslexia are discussed in more detail in Chapter 10.

The third reason for the lack of consensus over a definition is that the search for a consensus may have been hindered unwittingly by researchers having often taken many different theoretical perspectives. Each kind of research has emphasised different aspects of the problem in its definition. Depending on the type of research, resulting definitions have placed emphasis on either causal factors or descriptive ones. The chapter continues by summarising three major theoretical research perspectives that have been responsible for different definitions.

Three theoretical research perspectives

The three different theoretical research perspectives of dyslexia can be grouped into neurological/biological, cognitive and educational; each reflecting a different research interest. Various definitions have been postulated by special interest groups such as the Dyslexia Association, the British Psychological Society, the International Dyslexia Association, etc., as well as by individual authors. These resulting definitions incorporate the research findings with varying degrees of emphasis placed on the various research findings. While having enhanced our general understanding of dyslexia these three research perspectives may have contributed to no consensus to date on a definition of dyslexia. Attempts to accommodate these research perspectives into a single definition of dyslexia continue to prove difficult. It is no wonder that professionals as well as non-specialists in this field have been confused.

A review of the research findings outlined in the previous chapter illustrated the different perspectives on dyslexia taken by researchers. The focus on separate aspects of the multi-faceted concept of dyslexia has almost inevitably led to the postulating of multiple theories of dyslexia. It is not surprising to discover that divergent theories have each produced their own definitions. An analysis of the definitions that have been generated by interest groups can be divided into two major categories of definition. These are causal and descriptive and are summarised below.

Causal and descriptive definitions of dyslexia

As suggested, it seems that the various researchers are all looking at the same phenomenon of dyslexia from their own perspective. Further analysis of subsequent definitions generated by specific interest groups and individuals reveals that these definitions could be grouped into causal and descriptive aspects of dyslexia. Varying emphasis is placed on these two specific aspects of dyslexia according to the different interests of particular official bodies, or authors of the proposed definition. This is further explained below.

Causal definitions

This type of definition has emerged from the research into the neurological and biological causes of dyslexia. It has been concerned mainly with the role played by brain functioning and is concerned with deficits in the ways in which some people interpret and process information that comes in through the senses. The focus in this type of research has been on identifying abnormalities and deficits in brain functioning, mainly using the fMRI technique. The research into a genetic basis for dyslexia would also come into this category. Researchers under this category have traditionally focused on a search for the causes of dyslexia.

Descriptive definitions of dyslexia

Research under this category would be the research into the processing of information received through the senses. Definitions have focused on difficulties with the processes of writing, reading, spelling and general organisation of everyday tasks and would rely on the measurement of literacy attainments. Research into levels of cognitive functioning such as phonological processing would also come under this category. This would also include the research into working memory.

Current definitions of dyslexia

Six popular definitions of dyslexia as delineated by official committees, organisational groups and individual professionals are given below. These definitions are presented with critical analysis to demonstrate their use of causal and descriptive properties. The definitions are also presented to demonstrate the lack of a current consensus in the definition of dyslexia and their lack of applicability to both children and adults.

1 The World Federation of Neurology (1968)

This definition was one of the first definitions of dyslexia that included both causal and descriptive factors perspectives of the research.

Dyslexia is a disorder in children who, despite conventional classroom teaching experience, fail to attain the language skills of reading, writing and spelling commensurate with their intellectual abilities.

The word disorder implies a medical abnormality which is clearly considered by the authors of this definition to be the cause of dyslexia. The definition also includes a descriptive type of definition when referring to educational attainments. However, there is no reference to adult dyslexia in this definition.

2 The International Dyslexia Association (IDA)

This definition is a further example of a definition that incorporated both causal and descriptive aspects. It also takes the view that dyslexia is mainly caused by a neurological abnormality. It is perhaps more inclusive of the symptoms of dyslexia than the previous definition presented above but would still not appropriately describe the adult with dyslexia.

Dyslexia is a specific learning disability that is neurological in origin. It is characterised by difficulties with accurate and /or fluent word recognition and by poor spelling and decoding abilities. These difficulties typically result from a deficit in the phonological component of language that is often unexpected in relation to other cognitive abilities and the provision of effective classroom instruction. Secondary consequences may include problems in reading comprehension and reduced reading experience can impede growth of vocabulary and background knowledge.

3 British Dyslexia Association (BDA)

This is the first definition to recognise that dyslexia may produce strengths as well as weaknesses.

It is a descriptive definition of dyslexia. It does not attempt include possible neurological or biological causes of dyslexia.

Dyslexia is best described as a combination of abilities and difficulties that affect the learning process in one or more of reading, spelling writing. Accompanying weaknesses may be identified in areas of speed of processing, short term memory, sequencing and organisation, auditory and/or visual perception, spoken language and motor skills. It is particularly related to mastering and using written language, which may include alphabetic, numeric and musical notation. Some dyslexics have outstanding creative skills. Others have strong oral skills. Some have no outstanding talents. They all have strengths. Dyslexia can occur despite normal; intellectual ability and teaching. It is independent of socioeconomic or language background.

The BDA definition makes no reference to the more complex difficulties faced by the adult as opposed to the child with dyslexia. Also, as it stands, it could apply equally to people with a general learning difficulty. It is not clear that this definition refers to a specific learning difficulty.

4. Dyslexia Action (Formerly the British Dyslexia Institute)

This definition dyslexia of dyslexia again encompasses both causal and descriptive definitions and is inclusive of most of the difficulties faced by a dyslexic child. Once again, however, it would not necessarily apply to adults with dyslexia.

Dyslexia causes difficulties in learning to read, write and spell. Short-term memory, mathematics, concentration, personal organisation and sequencing may also be affected. Dyslexia usually arises from a weakness in the processing of language-based information. Biological in origin, it tends to run in families, but environmental factors also contribute. Dyslexia can occur at any level of intellectual ability. It is not the result of poor motivation, emotional disturbance, sensory impairment or lack of opportunities, but it may occur alongside any of these. The effects of dyslexia can be largely overcome by skilled specialist teaching and the use of compensatory strategies.

As with the BDA definition, it is an optimistic definition, recognising that dyslexics often have strengths as well as weaknesses. However, this definition appears to be over optimistic, especially when considering adults with dyslexia. The basis of this statement is the belief that dyslexia can be overcome. It is agreed that compensatory strategies can help but from available evidence most dyslexics will always have weaknesses in short term memory that can continue to affect their lives in general.

5. British Psychological Society (BPS)

This is a wholly descriptive definition and notable for its brevity. It may be deliberately brief with the purpose of providing a practical definition that avoids reference to possible causes of dyslexia.

Dyslexia is evident when accurate and fluent word reading and/or spelling develops very incompletely or with great difficulty.

This BPS definition is narrow and although it may well have its uses when applied to children it most certainly does not adequately define the problem faced by adults. Moreover, as with the BDA definition, it does not distinguish between children with a general learning difficulty as opposed to those with a specific learning difficulty.

6 Individual Professionals

McLoughlin, *et al,* (2002) provide a further example of a definition that comprises both causal and descriptive aspects of the problem.

Developmental dyslexia is a genetically inherited and neurologically determined inefficiency in working memory, the information processing system fundamental to performance in conventional educational and work settings. It has a particular impact on verbal and on written communication as well as on organisation, planning and adaptation to change.

This definition is probably the most accurate and concise definition of dyslexia to date. It properly describes the difficulties experienced as being underpinned by a weakness in working memory. It also includes possible neurological and genetic determinants. It also accurately refers to the manifestations of the problem in literacy performance. Finally, it is a definition that could be usefully applied to both children and adults. However, although this definition focuses on working memory as a major factor in dyslexia, it does not distinguish between those with a general learning difficulty and those with a specific learning difficulty.

Reconciling the different definitions

The above definitions of dyslexia have all been criticized. These criticisms fall into two areas. Firstly, apart from McLaughlin, *et al*, (2002) definition, they all clearly refer to dyslexia as a childhood condition with no reference to adult dyslexia. The fact that the challenges faced by adults with dyslexia are more complex than those faced by children is ignored in these other definitions. As emphasised by McLoughlin, *et al*, dyslexia in the adult is rarely manifested solely by literacy difficulties. Although some dyslexic adults have difficulties with spelling and may be slow to read, the problems faced by the adult with dyslexia are much more complex. While a child's main focus is on learning the basic literacy skills, the adult with dyslexia is learning how to function in the wider social world. In contrast with the child, finance, employment and communication are areas in which the adult is expected to display competence. All of these areas can present particular problems to the adult with dyslexia that are not presented to the child.

The second major criticism is that, apart from the *IDA* definition, the above definitions do not differentiate between those people with a general learning difficulty and those with a specific learning difficulty. It is claimed in this book that an accurate definition of dyslexia should comprise not only the two types of definition included in other definitions as reported above, but a third theoretical perspective - the discrepancy definition. The discrepancy referred to is the presence of a significant discrepancy between working memory and reasoning ability. Evidence for this argument is provided in the next two sections. An explanation of working memory will be presented before going on to critically describe the significance of a discrepancy between working memory and reasoning ability.

Working memory

Working memory refers to the store of images, events and ideas transmitted through the five senses that comprise the human memory. The concept of memory is one of the most highly researched and complex areas of investigation in the field of psychology. There are many models postulated to explain different kinds of memory. However, the primary division of memory is into short-term and long-term memory. Both short-term and long-term memory involve the storing of information. Memory traces from both can be brought into consciousness without doing anything with the information. However, when short-term memory is activated and is involved in processing information it is referred to as 'working memory'. Further to this, it is important to take into account that working memory can be assessed in both the auditory and visual spheres of mental activity. Visual working memory is usually assessed through tasks that require the ability to match patterns and to recognise shapes. Examples of these tasks are to be found in *Chapter 5* when describing how to test for dyslexia.

An example of working memory in the auditory sphere would be the process involved when engaged in mental arithmetic. The successful completion of a mental arithmetic problem involves several intellectual tasks. It is necessary to be able to record the information through the auditory receptors, to understand the information, to retain the information, to manipulate the information, and finally to verbally express the answer. Both auditory short-term memory and intelligence are involved when completing a mental arithmetic problem. This is why an assessment of mental arithmetic ability is a useful part of an assessment for possible dyslexia.

Most researchers would recognise a weakness in working memory as a common characteristic of dyslexia. This holds true even if they differ in the prominence that they give to the weakness in working memory in arriving at a definition of dyslexia.

Intelligence in a definition of dyslexia.

As with the study of memory, it is recognised that the concept of intelligence is a massive area of research in the field of psychology. In particular, its definition has often been debated. This book takes the view that intelligence is a measure of logical reasoning ability in both the verbal and the non-verbal spheres of intellectual functioning. As with working memory, a measurements of intelligence would seem to be a necessary part of an assessment investigating possible dyslexia.

Since the work of Stanovich and Stanovich (1997) arguments for including intelligence in a definition of dyslexia have been rightly criticised. Mile and Miles (1989) wrote that a person at any level of intelligence may have a specific learning difficulty such as dyslexia. However, it is suggested in this book that there are grounds for the inclusion of intelligence in a dyslexia definition but only in relation to working memory abilities. In the Lawrence study (2009), 97% of the sample had a discrepancy between their working memory scores and their non-verbal intelligence scores, and 96% had a discrepancy between their working memory and their verbal intelligence scores.

Working memory and reasoning ability

Reasoning ability, or intelligence, needs to be observed in relation to a weakness in working memory before using the term dyslexia. For dyslexia, the weakness in working memory should be a *specific* difficulty and not part of an overall general learning difficulty. If both working memory and reasoning ability were weak then the term *general learning difficulty* would probably more accurately describe the difficulties.

The significance of a discrepancy between working memory and reasoning ability would appear to be pivotal in the formation of a definition of dyslexia. Further support for this notion is illustrated in a study conducted by the author of 447students in further and higher education (Lawrence 2009). This sample of students had been referred between April 1996 and October 2004 for testing for possible dyslexia. The majority of these referrals were made following various college screening procedures that had shown the students had difficulties with academic work. Subsequent testing on the *Wechsler Adult Intelligence Scales* revealed that 88% of the students assessed as having a significant discrepancy between scores on subtests measuring working memory and scores on subtests tests measuring intelligence. The remaining 12% were seen to have other reasons for their learning difficulties. Some of these other difficulties included lack of ability, motivational factors, scotopic sensitivity or emotional problems. It was after this analysis that it was strongly asserted that a definition of dyslexia should include the discrepancy between working memory and reasoning ability. The percentage differences between the different indexes are presented in *Appendix 6.*

There appears to be one significant area of intellectual functioning in the assessment of dyslexia that is common to both the adult and the child. This is the discrepancy between reasoning ability and working memory. In the definition proposed in this book, for a child, or an adult, to be described as being dyslexic, they would both have to show a significant difference between their reasoning ability and their working memory. This discrepancy is advocated as being an essential part of a universally applicable definition of dyslexia and would be referred to as a discrepancy definition.

Speed of processing in a definition of dyslexia

Slowness to process visual information is seen to be common characteristic of dyslexia. In the Lawrence study referred to above 95.5% were seen to be slow to process information, either in the visual sphere, or in the auditory sphere. Furthermore, this 93% had a discrepancy between their *Speed of Processing* scores and their verbal intelligence score. 96% had a discrepancy between their non-verbal intelligence and their *Processing Speed* score. There are many possible reasons why people may be slow to process information. Confused laterality, for example, is seen to be a common characteristic of dyslexia and causes a slight delay whenever having to process visual information that requires a decision to select left or right.. Visual stress (Singleton, 2008) is also likely to affect speed of processing. It is suggested, therefore, that the speed of processing visual information should also be included in a definition of dyslexia.

Visual discomfort and/or confused laterality is sometimes also responsible for a student being slow to process information. Students with Irlen Syndrome are likely to be slower than expected when processing visual information, such as writing. Those with confused laterality are also likely to be slower than expected, especially if they are processing visual tasks such as writing or copying from an overhead projector. In the Lawrence study quoted above 95.05% of students with either confused laterality of with the Irlen Syndrome were slow to process information

Dyslexia defined

In the light of the foregoing research and the various theories of dyslexia that have emerged, the following definition of dyslexia is suggested.

Dyslexia is a specific learning difficulty of neurological and biological origin that is most often characterised by a significant discrepancy between measures of working memory and reasoning ability together with a slowness in the speed of processing information that is usually manifested in a variety of educational attainments, particularly literacy skills, as well as in everyday tasks. .

There are five significant features that meet the criticisms that prevented previous definitions from gaining universal acceptance.

The five significant features are listed below:

1)Causal, descriptive and discrepancy definitions of dyslexia are included.

2)It is based on significant research findings.

3)The different theoretical research perspectives are reflected.

4)It reconciles previous definitions of dyslexia.

5)This definition would apply equally to children and to adults.

The task of obtaining a consensus on a definition of dyslexia has often been made difficult by the existence of other related conditions such as dyscalculia, scotopic sensitivity syndrome, dyspraxia, etc. that are often subsumed under the umbrella of dyslexia.

However, to be accurate and also to be useful, it is suggested that a definition of dyslexia should exclude these other related conditions. The definition of dyslexia suggested here does not include these other specific learning difficulties.

Summary

The lack of a consensus in a definition of dyslexia was discussed in this chapter. The chapter began with suggestions why there has been to date no consensus on a definition. Three possible reasons for this lack of a consensus were discussed. These reasons included the multi-faceted nature of dyslexia, the problem of trying to arrive at a definition acceptable for both children and adults, and the different research perspectives. It was suggested that the significant research into dyslexia could be grouped under causal and descriptive definitions of dyslexia. The popular current theories of dyslexia were presented with a critique of them all. An argument was presented to include in a definition of dyslexia, a significant discrepancy between working memory and intelligence to distinguish dyslexia from a general learning difficulty. Working memory was defined. The chapter concluded by offering a new definition of dyslexia that would incorporate discrepancy, causative and descriptive factors and be applicable to both children and adults.

In conclusion, despite a lack of consensus over how best to define dyslexia, there is universal agreement that there is an identifiable group of people that experience specific learning difficulties in the development and expression of literacy and language skills. There is also agreement that these difficulties are often inherited and neurologically based. It is also seems that most dyslexics demonstrate a weakness in working memory. There is general agreement that the term dyslexia should be used to describe this group. Furthermore, it is also agreed that these difficulties persist in various forms throughout life. However, when considering the different published definitions of dyslexia they are all either too narrow or too wide and usually would apply only to children with dyslexia. The view taken here is similar to the definition proposed by McLoughlin, *et.al.* and, adds that that a definition of dyslexia should also include a significant discrepancy between working memory and reasoning ability as manifested in everyday tasks, including literacy and should also apply to adults as well as to children.

Chapter 4
What tests are used to identify dyslexia?

Introduction

Lecturers and tutors often ask whether there are any tests they might use themselves to identify those who might be dyslexic without needing to refer the student to a specialist for an assessment. The answer to this question is that there are tests that can be used by non-specialists as well as types of screening procedures.

Apart from formal tests, tutors, lecturers and others who regularly come into contact with students can have an important part to play in identifying symptoms of dyslexia. Tutors and lecturers are often the first to witness symptoms. Tutors in further education and those in basic education classes who are involved in the teaching of basic educational skills tend to identify possible dyslexic students very quickly as obviously their main focus is on literacy. Chapter 4 begins by discussing the role played by tutors and lectures in identifying symptoms of dyslexia.

The various methods available for the screening of dyslexia are outlined in this chapter. This is followed by a discussion of the limitations of some of these screening procedures.

It is essential that a further interview with the student is arranged after the screening to discuss the results and to provide general reassurance to the student. The format of the interview is discussed in this chapter.

The format and the content of a psychological assessment can in itself be a source of anxiety, particularly if it is suggested that the student be assessed by a psychologist. An assessment for dyslexia by a qualified teacher may not necessarily arouse the same degree of anxieties. The title 'educational psychologist' can be a source of anxiety. Whereas people in general are aware of the role of a teacher, most people tend to be unsure of the role of an educational psychologist. The importance of reassuring the student's anxieties surrounding the referral to a psychologist is discussed in this chapter. The qualifications and the role of the educational psychologist are outlined.

The chapter ends by explaining why an educational psychologist is often preferred to conduct the detailed psychological assessment.

The lecturer/tutor role in identifying possible dyslexia

Although many students have had their dyslexia diagnosed before entering adult education, there are many others who are unaware that they are dyslexic until after they have entered adult education. It is not until they begin to struggle with their studies that dyslexia is suspected. Obviously, not all students who struggle with their studies have dyslexia. There are many reasons apart from dyslexia why students can have difficulties with their work. Amongst the most common reasons for a student's learning difficulties are problems of motivation, emotional stress, or simply lack of ability. As discussed in the previous chapter, there are also other common learning difficulties that can easily be confused with dyslexia. However, when a student is seen to be having difficulties with academic work and there is no obvious reason for it, it would not be unreasonable for the tutor or lecturer to consider dyslexia.

Lecturers and tutors who are in frequent contact with students are often the first to identify the student with dyslexia. This most often occurs when marking the submission of a student's written work. Common signs of possible dyslexia might include poor spelling, ungrammatical sentences and an apparent disorganisation in the way their ideas are expressed. A further reason for suspecting dyslexia would be where there appears to be a discrepancy between the poor quality of the student's written work and the student's oral responses in class discussion groups where they may be slow to respond. Word retrieval is often slow for those with dyslexia.

Once the tutor or lecturer has grounds to suspect dyslexia there are steps they might take before deciding to refer the student for a detailed psychological assessment. The first step for the lecturer would be to discuss their concerns with the student. The next step would normally be to suggest to the student that they seek an interview with the college student support services, where they are available. The student might then relate other type of difficulties that they have experienced, perhaps including more symptoms of dyslexia, as outlined in Chapter 1. The suggestion might then be made to the student that it would be advisable for them to have a formal screening procedure to investigate the possibility of dyslexia. These are described in the following sections.

Check list of symptoms of dyslexia

Many educational institutions prefer to administer a checklist of symptoms to students before referring them for a more detailed diagnostic assessment. Many of these checklists are compiled by the particular institution and comprise a list of possible symptoms of dyslexia as discussed in chapter one. There are many forms of such checklists available for this purpose and an example of one of these is given in Appendix One.

In the usual check list, the student is asked to place a tick next to each symptom if they feel that the particular symptom applies to them. Whether dyslexia is suspected depends on how many symptoms are ticked. The greater the number of symptoms ticked, the more likely that the student has dyslexia.

Check lists are particularly useful in discovering whether the student does indeed show symptoms of dyslexia. Where the check list does not indicate symptoms of dyslexia the student's difficulties would need to be investigated further through other means. This investigation may require an interview with a psychologist. When the possibility of dyslexia is first suggested some students find it hard to accept that may have dyslexia. The filling in of a check list can have the necessary and desirable effect of helping them to become more aware of their problems and help them become used to the possibility of dyslexia. If they find that they have many of the symptoms listed on the checklist they are more likely to accept the need for a psychological assessment to confirm dyslexia.

Where the check list confirms symptoms of dyslexia a psychological assessment is usually arranged to investigate the condition in more detail. This would not only be for the purpose of confirming the dyslexia but also to make recommendations on how best to help the student.

Some lecturers may be uncertain whether the difficulties shown by the student in their academic work are sufficiently severe to take the step of recommending a detailed psychological assessment. In this case, the preliminary step of filling in a checklist is a particularly useful first step.

Self-administered computer programmes

Many students with dyslexia become anxious when having to fill in forms, especially in public. Even though the form is designed to help them, as in the case of a dyslexia checklist, they can easily become confused. This is where a self-administered screening procedure that can be completed in privacy is particularly useful. Some colleges administer routine screening procedures for all students on first entering college. In these cases it would not necessarily be the lecturer or tutor who would be the first to identify symptoms of dyslexia.

The various self-administered computer programmes available are more sophisticated than checklists. In contrast to checklists, self-administered computer programmes usually consist of a series of questions and tasks for which norms are available. 'Norms' are statistical measures showing the average test scores obtained when the test was devised and standardised. The norms usually comprise average test scores of a previously obtained sample of people of different ages. It is possible therefore to interpret a person's test score in terms of how far their result is above or below the average score, or norm, for their particular age.

Not all these self-administered computer programmes consist of tasks to be completed. Many programmes are similar to the norm-free checklists in that they also consist of a series of questions to which the student has to give a positive or a negative answer.

The self-administered computer based testing programme has become increasingly popular because it is quick and easy to administer. The more useful self-administered computer programmes also contain a variety of tests of cognitive abilities. One example of a computer programme is the STUDYSCAN (Zdienski, 1997) and is in two parts. The first part of the test comprises a full battery of tests including tests of working memory, intelligence and literacy attainments. A major criticism of this battery of tests is that some of the language used may be difficult to interpret for students with literacy difficulties.

Part two of the test, known as Quick Scan, comprises a short questionnaire to identify learning styles. As discussed in the previous chapter, it has been hypothesised by some writers that a person who is dyslexic would be more likely to prefer a specific learning style. It is hypothesised that dyslexics would show a higher range of abilities in the visuo-spatial sphere as opposed to the verbal sphere. Although research may ultimately show this to be a valid procedure, as discussed in the previous chapter the evidence for the validity of this approach has yet to be established. However, several educational institutions have introduced computer screening tests like the STUDYSCAN as a routine screening procedure for all new entrants.

As well obviating the need to write, another reason why students often prefer a computer, self-administered programme such as the Study Scan is that they it does ensure confidentiality of results. This is important for some students who may be embarrassed by their learning difficulties.

Individual testing programmes

Although there is a place for both the check list and the computer testing programme as a method of preliminary screening, a testing programme administered on a one-to-one basis is usually better standardised and so more reliable. Amongst the more popular individual testing programmes are the Dyslexia Adult Screening Test (DAST) (Fawcett and Nicholson, 1998) and the Bangor Dyslexia Test (Miles, 1982). The Bangor Dyslexia Test was designed for use with children from seven years of age up to the age of eighteen and is designed to identify symptoms of dyslexia. This is an excellent screening device where time is limited. However, the test designed by Fawcett and Nicholson is not only designed to assess symptoms of dyslexia but also gives an estimate of reasoning ability and provides a profile of strengths as well as weaknesses. It is useful to be able to obtain an estimate of students' strengths as well as their possible weaknesses. The DAST comprises 11 subtests in all and notably avoids the compilation of the traditional IQ as discussed in Chapter 6. A major limitation of this test is that it does not give an estimate of the student's visual processing that is so often weak in dyslexic people.

The DAST is particularly useful for dyslexic adults as the test results can be depicted graphically making it easier to understand. Where the results show a discrepancy between working memory and intelligence a further detailed psychological testing would normally be arranged.

An intelligence test originally devised and standardised by John Raven (1998) is a popular test that is not on restricted usage so can be used by people other than psychologists. The *Raven's Progressive Matrices* has been used world-wide for the last thirty years and its popularity continues. This test is particularly useful for dyslexic students as it is relatively unaffected by language difficulties. It consists of a series of pages each containing a visual pattern with a piece missing. The task is to find the missing piece from a series of other patterns. It is said to provide a measure of general intellectual ability but is probably best considered as a test of non-verbal ability. The test can be administered either with or without a time limit and usually takes about thirty minutes to complete. Results are recorded in centiles. (See Chapter 6 for interpretation of centiles).

Limitations of preliminary screening procedures.

Although there is a place for screening devices they are all subject to various criticisms. Their results should always be interpreted with care. The first criticism leveled at these procedures is that they can give both false positive and false negative results. This means that the results can show that people are dyslexic when, in fact, they may not be dyslexic and also the converse; they may show that people are not dyslexic when in fact they are dyslexic. People with dyslexia can demonstrate a variety of symptoms but some adults, through practice and experience over many years, have learned to compensate for their dyslexia. These are the people who may not show up as being dyslexic on a screening test.

Checklists of symptoms are particularly subject to this criticism. Also, some people may show few symptoms of dyslexia as a result of intense practice or expert tuition. However, they may still have other symptoms not listed in the checklist so their dyslexia would be missed. For instance, they might need extra time in examinations to process information. The checklist would be showing what is known as a 'false negative'. This does not mean that the person who has learned to compensate for their condition is no longer dyslexic

Although many of the self-administered computer programmes are more reliable than checklists, they still do not possess the same levels of reliability and validity as a one-to-one testing situation. Self-administered testing of abilities is renowned for being less reliable than individual testing. The main reason for the relatively lower level of reliability of a self-administered test is that any testing of abilities requires the subject to be relaxed and properly motivated. Many people with dyslexia find prolonged concentration difficult and it is only within an individual test session that the student can be encouraged to persevere. The skill of the assessor is a key factor in ensuring adequate motivation and a relaxed testing environment. Research has consistently shown that it is possible to obtain more reliable test results with individual testing than is possible with a self-administered test. The same criticism would apply to group testing.

An important criticism of screening devices is that dyslexia can often be confused with other kinds of learning difficulty. Many of the conditions discussed in chapter two that show similar symptoms to dyslexia can easily show up on a checklist as dyslexia. For instance, a person who has been showing symptoms of Attention Deficit Hyperactivity Disorder (ADHD) would find themselves giving positive replies to many of the questions on the checklist such as, 'Do you find prolonged concentration difficult?' or 'Do you easily forget oral instructions?' Only an individual testing with appropriate materials and administered by a qualified professional, could accurately differentiate between the person with ADHD and the person who is dyslexic.

As with the use of the checklist of symptoms, the computerised programme designed to assess learning style is not always a reliable or a definitive diagnostic tool. The reason for this is that research into learning styles has produced conflicting evidence about the exclusive use of any one learning style in an individual's repertoire. This research leans towards the conclusion that people do not habitually use one learning style but use different learning styles at different times.

It should be emphasised that if the student considers applying for the entitled Disability Allowance for the purchase of equipment, the results of a screening procedure would not always satisfy eligibility requirements. A psychological assessment would almost certainly be required. Most education authorities continue to require either a psychologist's report or one from a teacher who is particularly qualified in the assessment of dyslexia.

Interviewing the student after the screening

Where the results of any of the screening devices described above indicate possible dyslexia, they should always be supplemented by a discussion with the student to explain the results and the need for a possible further psychological assessment. The main aim of the interview is to provide support and reassurance regarding the meaning of dyslexia and if the dyslexia is confirmed, its possible consequences for academic study. It should also be explained to the student when discussing the screening results that it should not be automatically assumed that dyslexia is now confirmed. The view taken should be that 'there are grounds for concern' that warrant further investigation. It would be necessary to obtain permission from the student before arranging a fuller psychological testing.

In the past, a psychological assessment had to be conducted by a psychologist but recent developments in testing and training courses in testing have seen the emergence of the specialist teacher also qualified to do the assessment. In practice, the decision on who to approach to do the further assessment generally depends on which kind of professional is available.

Once their permission has been given, it should be explained to the student that any relevant information they could provide on their background would be potentially useful in the final assessment. It would be important to know, for instance, whether the student had had similar difficulties when at school and whether they had received a previous assessment. Further information of a medical, educational and psychological nature would also be gathered. Any head injuries or sensory defects may be additional evidence for dyslexia. Although the evidence would point to there being a genetic factor in dyslexia, a head injury at any stage may produce symptoms of dyslexia. If the interview reveals that there has been a head injury and that the learning difficulties started soon afterwards this would be important information to impart to the psychologist. As dyslexia is usually different in each case it is important to obtain as full a picture of the student as possible to assist in the identification of dyslexia and subsequent recommendations for treatment.

Students who appear to show symptoms of dyslexia for the first time usually receive the news of the screening results with mixed feelings. Some will be shocked; others will simply become bemused by the term. Almost all will experience a degree of anxiety about the possible confirmation of dyslexia. A major reason for this anxiety is that their knowledge of dyslexia is usually scanty so it is imperative that the interviewer takes time to explain to them what dyslexia means. They will want reassurance that it will not affect their grades. They will want to know whether the label 'dyslexia' will be on their records when seeking employment in the future. These concerns need to be addressed.

After having obtained an appropriate history from the student, the remainder of the interview would generally consist of gathering information from the student regarding the precise nature of their difficulties with the course work. In making a referral for a detailed psychological assessment, it would be helpful to know what it is that the student perceives as their main difficulties and how they feel about them.

The student should be reassured about the psychological referral by explaining to them what is involved in the assessment. The interviewer would need to help the student understand the kind of help they could expect to receive from the psychologist or the specialist teacher conducting the assessment. While most students usually understand the role of the specialist teacher they may not be so familiar with the work of a psychologist. It is not unnatural for some students to be anxious about seeing a psychologist for the assessment. Just as with the concept of dyslexia itself, many people are unsure exactly what to expect from a psychologist. Knowing how an educational psychologist is trained helps them to understand their role better and also helps to reduce any anxieties about the assessment. It is reassuring to the student to be made aware of the qualifications of the psychologist and the way in which the psychologist will work in the forthcoming interview.

Qualifications of an educational psychologist

The training of an educational psychologist takes a minimum of seven years. The first part of their training is a university course leading to a degree in psychology. The next step for new graduates in psychology who wish to qualify as educational psychologists would be to obtain a teaching qualification.

An educational psychologist normally has to be a trained teacher as well as a psychologist. The teacher training is normally followed by a minimum of two years successful teaching. Until recently their final qualification was a post-graduate degree in educational psychology. Universities are now beginning to offer a three-year full time training to doctorate level. This is followed by obtaining a post in a local authority psychological service where the psychologist will be working under supervision. Once the period of supervision is completed the psychologist is eligible to apply for Chartered Status and can apply for a Practicing Certificate issued by the British Psychological Society. The educational psychologist is now qualified to practice.

A qualified psychologist would be an educational psychologist whose name appears on the Chartered List of Psychologists, maintained and published by the British Psychological Society (BPS). The aim of this document is to protect the public from employing a psychologist who may attempt to work in this applied area of psychology, without possessing the necessary qualifications. Copies of the document are available in Public Libraries throughout the UK. The psychologists named in this document would have the letters C.Psychol placed after their names. There are stringent regulations governing the use of these letters and only those with approved BPS training are eligible to use them.

Adult dyslexia as a specific area of expertise for the educational psychologist

Most educational psychologists' work is with children but not all educational psychologists are experienced in assessing adults with dyslexia. In the first place, different test materials are used. The ways in which dyslexia are manifested are different in the adult from that in the child, as was discussed in Chapter 1.

The work of an educational psychologist is greatly varied and the topic of assessing for dyslexia in adults is only one area of specialism. It would be rare for an educational psychologist to agree to an assessment of adults for dyslexia without adequate training or appropriate experience in this area. However, it is the responsibility of the agency that arranges the assessment to ensure that the psychologist contracted to see their students possesses the necessary qualifications and experience with the testing of adults.

The value of employing the educational psychologist for the assessment

There are three important reasons why a dyslexia diagnostic assessment carried out by a qualified educational psychologist is often preferred. Firstly, as mentioned earlier, there are many specialist teachers qualified in the field of dyslexia who are trained to administer pre-selected diagnostic tests. However, there are a myriad of other psychological tests available and some of these are on restricted usage which means that they are not available to these teachers. Amongst these restricted tests is the Wechsler Adult Intelligence Scales (WAIS). This test is probably the most commonly used by psychologists when assessing learning difficulties and is used by psychologists in all the English speaking countries throughout the world. The WAIS series of tests is the result of over 50 years of research and development and requires specialist training in its administration and interpretation. As such it is probably the most reliable and the best standardised tests of intellectual functioning available. Full details of these tests are given in the next chapter.

A second reason why many authorities prefer to employ the educational psychologist is because the specialist qualifications of the psychologists enable them to assess not only the student's intellect but also their emotional adjustment. As research continually indicates, a correlation between emotional and intellectual functioning can be a significant factor in the final assessment of dyslexia.

Thirdly, as discussed in the previous chapter, there are other learning difficulties that can be confused with dyslexia. It would be rare for the specialist teacher to be as equally familiar and experienced as the psychologist in the assessment of these other conditions.

It is the responsibility of the agency referring the student to ensure that the professional they approach for the assessment is properly qualified to conduct the assessment, whether this is a psychologist or a specialist teacher assessor.

Summary

This chapter answered the question posed by staff whether there are any tests available for identifying dyslexia without necessarily referring their students for a detailed psychological assessment. The various forms of screening procedures available for a preliminary assessment of possible dyslexia were described. These included checklists of symptoms, self-administered computer programmes and formal one-to-one testing procedures. The relative value and possible shortcomings of these procedures were discussed. The need for an interview with the students to explain the results of the screening was highlighted. It was explained that the interview would be necessary for several reasons. The interview would be opportunity to explain to the student the nature of dyslexia and to reassure the student regarding the need for a possible referral for a detailed psychological assessment for the purpose of gathering other relevant information. When referral to a psychologist is suggested, the role of a psychologist was outlined as a topic that also would need to be explained to the student. The details of a psychological assessment and the tests used are discussed in the next chapter.

Chapter 5
What tests do the psychologists use to confirm dyslexia?

Introduction

Most staff are curious to know what tests are used in the psychological assessment and how they differ from the ones they might use themselves. Also, they may need to reassure those students who are referred for a psychological assessment. It was recommended in the previous chapter that a detailed psychological assessment should follow a screening procedure once possible dyslexia has been identified. There are three main reasons for this recommendation. Firstly, there are other specific learning difficulties related to dyslexia that can be easily mistaken for dyslexia. A detailed psychological assessment would be able to identify these. A second reason for a psychological assessment is that although the screening procedure may have revealed specific weaknesses in cognitive abilities, most screening procedures are not normally designed to assess detailed intellectual functioning. The student's strengths as well as their weaknesses would be assessed in a detailed psychological assessment procedure.

A third reason for needing a psychological assessment is that sometimes an assessment of non-cognitive factors is relevant and screening devices are not normally designed to assess these. An assessment of self-esteem, locus of control, anxiety levels and general motivational states are often desirable. These factors can so easily influence the results of the cognitive testing. An assessment of the influence of non-cognitive factors is usually made in the light of the psychologist's clinical experience. Clinical judgment can also be supplemented if necessary by appropriate standardised tests. These reasons for recommending a detailed psychological assessment are discussed in this chapter.

Where the assessment is conducted by a psychologist, the current *Wechsler Adult Intelligence Scale III* (WAIS III) would most often form the basis of the detailed assessment. An overview of the WAIS III is presented in this chapter, describing each of the subtests and what they measure. Other tests used in the assessment, such as literacy tests and tests for laterality are also outlined in this chapter, together with tests of speed of writing.

The chapter begins with a discussion on the nature of intelligence.

The concept of intelligence

There has been voluminous research into the nature of intelligence over many years and it is probably true to say that this topic has been the object of more attention and more controversy than any other single topic in psychology. Intelligence testing in particular has been a vast area of research for decades, for both psychologists and educationalists. Many different definitions of intelligence have been offered and many different tests to measure intelligence have been developed. The *Wechsler Intelligence Test (III)* is probably the most used of all the tests of intelligence. Before describing this test it is necessary first to offer a definition of intelligence that would be useful when diagnosing dyslexia.

In order to define intelligence it may be helpful first to say what is 'not' intelligence. It is not an entity in the brain like a muscle that can be made bigger through training. Intelligence is not something that can be viewed under a microscope. In fact, it is probably more accurate to regard intelligence not as a 'thing' but more a way of behaving. So, it is probably better to refer to 'intelligent behaviour' rather than 'intelligence'. However, for simplicity sake we can still use the word intelligence.

In everyday life we all seem to know intuitively what we mean by intelligence. When we say a person is intelligent we are usually referring to several abilities. Amongst these abilities are the quality of their reasoning, their speed of thinking, their capacity for understand things quickly and their problem solving ability. These abilities can be manifested in either the verbal sphere or in the nonverbal sphere.

Consequently, separate measurements can be made of verbal intelligence and nonverbal intelligence. Psychologists have devised intelligence tests to measure both verbal and nonverbal problem solving behaviour. The tests are then administered to large samples of people of different age groups and average scores are then calculated for each age level. This makes it possible, when subsequently measuring an individual's intelligence, to compare their scores with the average scores of others of the same age.

A valid intelligence test is dependent on how far the tests really do measure what we mean by intelligent behaviour. This is known as the validity of the test and the degree of validity can be measured. Intelligence tests measure different things depending on the type of activities that are included in the tests. This is why defining intelligence has historically been difficult and has led to the view in some quarters that intelligence is simply 'what intelligence tests measure'. This may sound like a somewhat facetious definition of intelligence, but it also contains a grain of truth.

Although it is not possible to separate completely the effects of heredity from environment, there is strong evidence, through identical twin studies, that the greater part of what we mean by intelligence is inherited. However, although heredity may set the limits of the development of intelligent behaviour, there is no way of knowing *a priori* what those limits will be. In teaching, therefore, it is usually assumed that the limits of development of intelligence have not been reached. It used to be thought that intelligence was a fixed amount located somewhere in the brain and its amount would be fixed at birth. It is now known that intelligence test scores can increase on a retest after a period of intense intellectual stimulation. The converse can also happen; a person will show a decrease in scores after a prolonged period without intellectual stimulation. Clearly, environmental influences pay a significant part in the development of intelligence.

The Wechsler Adult Intelligence Scale (III) series of tests

As defined in Chapter 1, dyslexia is manifested in many different ways and the person with dyslexia can display weaknesses in several different intellectual functions. It is important, therefore, when assessing for dyslexia, to obtain measures of all these different aspects of intellectual functioning. In this way, a person's specific strengths as well as specific weaknesses can be identified. Most authorities would probably agree that the abilities are best measured by the *Wechsler Intelligence Scales (III)*. These tests comprise a series of subtests that measure an individual's performance in each of the two separate spheres of verbal and nonverbal intellectual functioning referred to earlier. Three separate intelligence quotients (IQs) can be calculated for verbal ability, nonverbal ability and for a full IQ that combines these two. The *Wechsler Adult Intelligence Scale III* (WAIS III) series of tests are now described.

The WAIS III is probably the best standardised, and the most reliable and valid test of adult intelligence available. It is in the forefront of most educational psychologist's battery of tests and would be used routinely by most psychologists when assessing learning difficulties. It has been revised several times since its inception in 1955 and has been standardised on large populations in both the United States and in Britain. The most recently revised version was published in 2002 and was updated for use with people aged from sixteen to eighty–nine.

There are fourteen test items in the WAIS III, divided into seven verbal tests and seven performance (nonverbal) tests. The fourteen tests each measure a different intellectual ability. Their results can be summed to obtain a global measure of intelligence. The individual test items and explanations of the abilities that they measure are listed below.

Verbal Tests

Vocabulary Test

This test requires definitions for a series of words presented orally and in order of increasing complexity. It reflects individual cultural experiences that include reading experience. It is also dependent on working memory.

Similarities Test

This test measures the ability to explain what two words have in common. It is measuring verbal concept formation and verbal reasoning ability.

Arithmetic Test

This test requires the solving of a series of arithmetic problems presented orally and with increased difficulty. The items are timed. The test is measuring working memory as the subject has to retain the information and then to be able to process it.

Digit symbol Test

This test consists of two lists of orally presented number sequences. Each number series is increasing in length. The subject is asked to recall the first series forwards and the second series backwards. It is measuring both auditory rote memory as well as auditory sequential memory.

Information Test

This test consists of a series of general knowledge questions presented orally about factual information. It reflects a person's cultural background and it is also a measure of long-term memory.

Comprehension Test

This test consists of a series of orally presented questions designed to measure the ability to obtain practical solutions in social situations.

It has been referred to as a test of common sense. As most of the questions are lengthy in their administration it also is dependent on working memory.

Letter-number sequence Test

This test consists of an orally presented series of numbers and a series of letters. The subject is asked to repeat the numbers and letters giving the numbers first in numerical order and the letters second in alphabetical order. Like the digit span test, it is a measure of working memory.

Performance nonverbal tests

Picture completion Test

This test consists of a series of coloured picture cards, each with an important part missing. The subject has to identify the missing piece. It is a measure of visual perception and attention to detail as well as a measure of long-term memory.

Digit symbol Test

This is a pencil and paper test. It consists of a series of numbers each of which has a blank square beneath it. The subject is given a key containing a symbol for each number. They are then asked to fill in the blank squares with the corresponding symbol from a key. The test is timed and is a measure of the speed of processing visual information, fine motor coordination and visual sequential memory.

Block Design Test

This test consists of nine coloured blocks. The subject is asked to construct geometric patterns with the blocks copied from designs presented on a separate card. The items of the test have to be completed within a specified time. It is a test of visuo-spatial organisation and visual problem solving. The literature considers this test to be a measure of nonverbal reasoning ability and the speed of processing visual information.

Matrix reasoning Test

This test consists of a series of cards each containing coloured patterns. Each of the patterns has one piece missing. The subject is asked which of a series of five other smaller patterns is the missing piece. This test is also considered to be a measure of nonverbal reasoning ability. Its successful performance is often adversely affected if the subject has any visual deficit or lateral confusion.

Picture arrangement Test

This test consists of a series of three to seven cards, each containing a cartoon picture. The subject is asked to arrange the cards in their logical sequence to tell a story in a fixed period of time. It is a test of visual sequential thinking.

Symbol search Test

This test consists of a series of five symbols at the end of which there are two other symbols. The subject is asked to mark 'Yes' or 'No', using a pencil, if either of the two symbols are seen to be present in the line of symbols. The test is timed and so is a measure of the speed of processing visual information. It is also reflects fine motor coordination ability.

Object assembly Test

This test requires the subject to complete a series of jigsaw puzzles of common objects. It is a measure of visuo-spatial organisation and the ability to form visual concepts.

Other cognitive tests used to diagnose dyslexia

Wechsler Memory Scales

Some psychologists might supplement the WAIS III with the *Wechsler Memory Scales* (WMS). These scales assess different aspects of memory and in much more detail than the memory subtests of the WAIS. When assessing for possible dyslexia, they would usually only be administered if there were some doubt about the scores obtained on the WAIS III and further clarification of the results was needed. If the WMS as well as the WAIS III are administered this would inevitably increase the testing time and so the full assessment would probably be spread over two sessions.

Phonological Assessment

Research has consistently shown a relationship between phonological processing ability and literacy skills. Phonology refers to the sound of words rather than to their meanings. The tests used to assess phonological skills are based on the premise that dyslexia is the result of a discrepancy in the ability to perceive and to process sounds in words. A battery of tests such as those devised by Frederickson, Frith and Reason (1997) can be used. However, these were originally standardised on a child population, so there are no norms for an adult population. However, phonological weaknesses are common in adults with dyslexia, so part of the battery of tests, such as the Spoonerisms Test can be useful when diagnosing dyslexia in adults. The Spoonerisms Test is particularly suitable for adults where the adult is asked to deliberately devise a spoonerism as for example when asked to exchange initial sounds in two words. E.g. 'car park' would become 'par cark'. This task can prove difficult for people with a weakness in phonological analysis ability. It is not uncommon to come across adults with dyslexia who tend to use spoonerisms in everyday life, much to their embarrassment.

Laterality Tests

Dyslexic people often tend to reverse letters and also sometimes reverse the order of words in sentences. People who show this characteristic are said to have a degree of lateral confusion. This behaviour is normal with children up to around the age of five or six years of age who will tend to use both left and right hands interchangeably. However, by the age of eight years most children have usually established dominance for one hand over the other. They will also have developed one eye more dominant than the other so that if looking through a telescope, for example, they would put it to the dominant eye. By the time they are adults most people will generally have learned to distinguish left from right. However, there is evidence that in adult dyslexics there is often a slight delay when having to do so. For instance, if asking a person with lateral confusion who is driving a motor-car to turn left, they might hesitate before they actually turn left. This confused laterality is manifested in academic work through being slow to process written work and also in the occasional reversal of the order of letters when spelling.

The assessment of possible lateral confusion is usually carried out informally in the psychological examination although there are standard tests of laterality available such as the *Harris Tests of Laterality* (1979). There are several ways in which laterality can be assessed. The subject is normally asked to perform a series of tasks that demand the choice of left or right. One of these tasks, for example would be to look through a hole in the middle of a piece of paper and then slowly to bring the paper onto their face while continuing to look through the hole. The task for the tester is to observe which eye the person uses when the paper is brought right onto their face. The eye chosen will be their dominant eye. Those who are dyslexic are likely to be unsure which eye to select and may show confusion. A further test for laterality might be to ask the subject to point with their left hand to their right ear and instruct them to do the opposite. Again, the person with lateral confusion will demonstrate a marked delay in choosing. Testing for laterality is usually supplemented by information from the student on their personal experiences in choosing left from right in every day life. If there is a problem in this area they usually report a delay when they have to choose as when instructed to turn left or right while driving. They may also report a tendency to reverse the order of letters or words.

Some people have a dominant eye that is opposite from their dominant hand. So for instance, they may have their left eye dominant but are right handed and vice versa. These people are described as being crossed laterals. It used to be thought that crossed laterals would show symptoms of dyslexia. It is now known that this is not so. In several studies investigating the topic, the results have been shown that there as many crossed lateral subjects amongst people with dyslexia as there are amongst those who are not dyslexic. It is confused laterality that is commonly associated with dyslexia and which causes a delay when having to select left from right.

Literacy tests

Tests of reading attainment, spelling attainment, speed of reading and speed of writing are usually administered when assessing for

possible dyslexia. Most adults with dyslexia have little trouble reading, although they may be slow to do so, particularly if asked to read out aloud. Spelling attainment however, is often below average. This is because spelling ability places demands on phonological abilities. It is important to know the person's precise levels of attainments in reading and spelling in order to determine if they require remedial help in these areas.

Reading attainment is usually measured in three different ways; word recognition, comprehension and speed. As dyslexics are usually slow at reading aloud they can become easily dismayed by this public display of their weakness. There is research evidence to show that people with dyslexia process reading quicker when reading silently than when having to read aloud. For this reason, a written comprehension test is sometimes administered where dyslexia is suspected. The *Watts-Vernon Reading Test* is one example of a suitable comprehension test for adults. This test consists of thirty-five sentences with the final word in each sentence omitted. The task is to select the missing word from five alternate choices.

Further examples of suitable tests for assessing word recognition and spelling in adults are *Spadafore Diagnostic Reading Tests, Wide Range Achievement Tests* (WRAT) and the *Woodcock Reading Mastery Test* (WRMT). The third edition of the WRAT, WRAT3, is the result of 60 years development and has two particularly useful features. First, it gives a measure of reading, spelling and arithmetic skills. Secondly, each of these three measures comes in two alternate forms. This means that each battery of tests can be administered before and after any teaching without having to repeat the same tests. The tests have been standardised on ages from 5 years to 75 years so can be administered to children and adults. Finally, an important feature of the WRAT3 is that the test results are quoted in standard scores with the same standard deviations as the WAIS III. This means that its results are often helpful if used in conjunction with the WAIS III results when planning a remediation programme.

Speed of reading and writing is often slow in dyslexic students and one of the most useful tests is the *Adult Reading Test* (Brooks, Everatt and Fidler, 2004) that measures not only attainments in reading and spelling but also speed of reading and speed of writing. It is generally considered that the average adult student would be able to write at the rate of twenty words per minute. However, speed of writing is usually much slower than this in people with dyslexia, as writing is so dependent on working memory. Speed of reading is also slow with people who have dyslexia. Reading speed can be assessed through the presentation of various lists of words. A quick estimate of speed reading only in adults is that compiled by Aaron and Baker (1991). In the Aaron and Baker, there are two lists of twenty words that have to be read aloud as fast as possible. The first list was standardised on adult students in technical education and the second list on adults in

higher education. The average speed for the two lists of words is 14 seconds and 12 seconds respectively.

Length of time taken for a full assessment

It is difficult to be precise regarding the time taken for a full assessment for possible dyslexia but normally it should take approximately between two and three hours. The time taken for an assessment will vary largely according to the speed of working, the intelligence of the person being tested and the degree of cognitive weaknesses shown.

It may occasionally be necessary to arrange a second assessment session. This might happen where the person being tested becomes unduly stressed or arrives in an unmotivated condition. In most assessment sessions, the psychologist will be aware of the need to establish rapport with the person being tested and so a second session would not be required. They would automatically be prepared for dealing with emotional stress and ensure that the person is sufficiently relaxed before beginning the testing. Nonetheless, the psychologist would need to assess the motivational state of the person being tested in order to ensure a reliable test result. In rare cases, it has been known for a person being tested to display emotions that are so incapacitating that the test session had to be abandoned. In such a case, the psychologist would need to assess the disruptive emotions in more depth and may administer more formal tests of the person's emotional state as well as their motivation. These tests, known as non-cognitive tests, would also be administered where it is know in advance that the person being tested is likely to be unduly emotional. Methods of assessing non-cognitive factors are discussed below.

Assessing non-cognitive factors

Non-cognitive is the term given to the emotional and motivational aspects of personality to distinguish them from the cognitive or intellectual aspects like intelligence and memory. A person's anxiety levels, their self-esteem and their locus of control are among these non-cognitive factors. There is research to indicate that all of these factors can affect test performance. It is these non-cognitive factors that determine how far a person will be properly motivated to perform well in the test.

There are many reasons why a person might not be properly motivated to obtain a reliable test result. For example, a person's anxiety level is known to contribute to their motivational state. It is recognised that a modicum of anxiety is necessary for the successful completion of any task. However, it is well known that too much anxiety interferes with clear thinking and also with memory.

There are other factors that can be measured that also can affect test results. It is one of the skills of testing to be able to identify these other factors and then to make allowances for them. For instance, a

temporary mood, test familiarity or undue fatigue will affect performance on intellectual tasks.

Some non-cognitive factors such as self-esteem and locus of control can be measured with standardised formal tests. However, when assessing for dyslexia these factors are more likely to be assessed through clinical judgement and general observation of the person's responses to the test session. The observation of behaviour during the testing is crucial in making a judgment of these factors. The non-cognitive factors that can influence the final test results are discussed below.

Self-esteem

A person's level of self-esteem is a major non-cognitive factor that can affect test results. There is ample research evidence indicating a correlation between a person's level of academic attainment and their self-esteem level. Consequently, it is always desirable to assess self-esteem. The main object of the dyslexia assessment is to obtain cognitive measures and the person being tested is subjected to intensive intellectual effort in the process. It may be unfair therefore to subject them also to additional formal self-esteem testing. This is why, in general, self-esteem would be more likely to be assessed intuitively and based on observed test behaviour. However, if there are strong grounds for believing that low self-esteem is markedly affecting test performance then a second session might have to be

arranged during which self-esteem would be formally assessed. A fuller discussion on the importance of self-esteem is found in Chapter 9.

Locus of control

Locus of control is another non-cognitive factor that can affect test results and which research show s to have a correlation with academic achievement. Locus of control refers to the extent to which a person feels responsible for their present behaviour and for their academic performance, or otherwise. This factor can be measured along a continuum with internal locus of control at one end of the continuum to external locus of control at the other end of the continuum. Those people who consider their behaviour and their performance to be the results of other factors outside themselves are said to be externally controlled. People who consider that they are responsible for their behaviour and their performance are said to internally controlled. Clearly extreme attitudes of both external control and of internal control would be unhealthy. Most people would be situated somewhere in the middle on this dimension although there are some people who score at the extremes of the continuum.

Once again, it would be unfair to routinely subject a person being tested for dyslexia to a formal testing of their locus of control, in addition to the cognitive testing. Accordingly, the psychologist would make a clinical judgment of the person's locus of control during the test session. However, if there is a suspected problem with locus of control then, as with the need to measure self-esteem, a second test session would have to be arranged.

Sample copy of psychologist's report

A sample copy of a psychologist's report on an adult assessed for dyslexia is located in Appendix Two.

Summary

This chapter began with the reasons why a detailed psychological assessment is recommended following the identification of symptoms of dyslexia. Emphasis was place on the fact that only a detailed psychological assessment can confirm that a student is dyslexic. This was followed by an explanation of the concept of intelligence and the need to measure intelligence when assessing dyslexia. Although many cognitive factors can be measured by a screening procedure, a psychologist would normally be employed to conduct a detailed assessment of intellectual functioning that included both verbal and non-verbal intelligence. Although the assessment would usually be conducted by a qualified educational psychologist, qualified specialist teachers in dyslexia are increasingly being employed. The WAIS (III) tests as the most often used in the psychologist's assessment to measure intelligence and other cognitive factors were outlined. Other cognitive tests, including those for assessing literacy and laterality, were also discussed.

Reference was made to the length of time required for the successful completion of the WAIS III. Other tests, of a non-cognitive nature, that often supplement the results of the WAIS III were also outlined in this chapter. These involve self-esteem, locus of control and anxiety. They can all contribute to motivation and so influence test results. As the WAIS assessment is a time-consuming and often lengthy procedure additional formal tests to measure non-cognitive factors are rarely used when assessing for dyslexia. Non-cognitive factors are generally taken into account by skilled observation of the student's behaviour during the testing on the WAIS (III). A discussion of these non-cognitive factors concluded the chapter.

Chapter 6
How do I interpret the psychological report?

Introduction

The interpretation of the psychological report is a regular source of discussion and debate amongst staff. Understanding a psychologist's report is not an easy task for people who are not familiar with psychological terms. It is not just the psychological terms and the statistics used that make it difficult. Part of the problem lies in the fact is that different psychologists do not always use the same terminology or even, in some cases, the same tests. It is hardly surprising therefore to discover that psychological reports are sometimes difficult to understand by non-specialists in this area.

It is true that psychologists can vary in the way they write their reports following an assessment. Even so, they do have a common language and usually employ the same tests and the same statistics to record the test results. A recent DfES (2005) working group has now issued guidelines recommending not only a standardised format for reporting test results but also recommendations for the tests that should be used. Psychologists and others who write reports for dyslexic adult students applying for a Disabled Students Allowance (DSA) are now expected to write their reports in this standardised format. The recommended format is presented in Appendix Two.

Following the assessment, the student's scores on the various tests are statistically collated and then presented in the report along with their interpretation. Test results of any non-cognitive factors that may have been assessed are also incorporated in the report. The special ways in which test scores are reported are discussed in this chapter.

Although the test results obtained from the administration of the WAIS(III) are usually collated to obtain an IQ, this method of calculation of results is not seen always to be meaningful when dyslexia is diagnosed. The traditional method of calculating an IQ from the WAIS tests results is recognised now as having its limitations when assessing for dyslexia. Accordingly, a more easily understood system of recording the WAIS III results has been devised without collating the traditional IQ. This procedure of recording test scores involves the calculation of four different measures of intellectual functioning, known as 'indexes'. These indexes are explained and discussed in this chapter.

The test results obtained from an assessment are often couched in unfamiliar statistical terms that can be confusing to staff who have not been trained in psychological measurement. The basic statistics used in the psychological report are explained in this chapter. It will be reassuring for staff to know that a detailed knowledge of statistical theory is not necessary in order to understand these statistics. Finally in this chapter, the need to record test behaviour and to record observations of non-cognitive factors is discussed.

The chapter begins with a discussion of the limitations of the traditional reporting of test results collated to obtain an Intelligence Quotient (IQ).

Limitations of the intelligence quotient

In the past, the WAIS(II) was invariably used to obtain an intelligence quotient (IQ) that was calculated by adding together the results of all the subtests. This method of recording test results when assessing for possible dyslexia is now seen to have limitations. The reason for this is that the intelligence of a person who was dyslexic would be underestimated by the use of a single IQ figure. An IQ is a composite of several subtests added together, including tests of vocabulary, general knowledge, memory, speed of processing information and measures of reasoning ability in both verbal and nonverbal modes.

In the person who is dyslexic, there is usually a significant discrepancy between scores on the tests of working memory and those obtained on tests of reasoning ability. A person who is dyslexic could have obtained above average scores on the subtests measuring intelligence but would have usually obtained below average scores on subtests measuring working memory. However, as all subtest scores are added together, the final IQ figure would be brought down by the inclusion of the lower working memory scores. The traditional IQ figure would tell the reader of the report nothing about this discrepancy.

Quoting an IQ need not be a problem if the reader of the report understands how the IQ is calculated. Unfortunately, it is not always appreciated that an IQ is calculated through summing all the subtest scores, with each measuring a different ability. When an IQ is reported without explanation of how the tester has arrived at the figure it can so easily cause distress for those students diagnosed as being dyslexic as well as confusing for professionals. The figure quoted is invariably below the level that they would have expected, giving a false impression of their intelligence level. Their intelligence is so easily misrepresented in this way.

Despite the risks of misinterpretation, the recording of the IQ is still warranted in particular circumstances. For example, it would be useful for providing necessary evidence in cases where the assessment did not indicate dyslexia. It would be useful to record an IQ where the testing reveals the presence of a general learning difficulty and not a specific learning difficulty. This would apply if the results of WAIS

III indicated that all test scores were below average with no indication of a specific weakness in any particular area of ability.

This problem of the possible misunderstanding of the IQ has been addressed in the recent revision of the WAIS. The misinterpretation of the person's intelligence is minimised by standardising the test items in a different way so that it is no longer necessary to quote an IQ. It is still possible to obtain an IQ from the WAIS III test results if this is required. However, the new version of the WAIS is standardised so that a measure of verbal and nonverbal intelligence can still be made but with their separation from other abilities tested. This is explained further below.

Four indexes as alternative to the IQ

There is provision in the recent revision of the WAIS for the calculation of four separate abilities. These are verbal intelligence, nonverbal intelligence, memory and speed of processing information. This is a particularly useful division in the process of arriving at a confirmation of dyslexia. When arriving at a diagnosis of dyslexia there is usually a significant discrepancy between the scores on subtests measuring intelligence and the scores measuring working memory

It is particularly important in the confirmation of dyslexia to report a person's strengths as well as their weaknesses. The discrepancy between the strengths and weakness has been made more obvious under this new method of calculation. It is reassuring for a person who is seen to have a weakness in working memory to know that their intelligence is at least within normal limits and may even be higher. It is also reassuring for them to know that the reason for their literacy difficulties is not lack of intelligence. Their strengths as well as specific areas of weakness can be identified more easily with the four indexes.

The four indexes comprise the results of particular subtests in the WAIS III. These subtests were all described in the previous chapter. The following description of the four indexes lists the subtests in each division.

1. The Verbal Comprehension Index (VCI)

The VCI is considered to be a valid measure of verbal intelligence. The scores that are to be added together to calculate this index are from the following subtests.

Vocabulary Subtest

Similarities Subtest

Information Subtest

2. The Perceptual Organisation Index (POI)

The POI is considered to be a valid measure of nonverbal intelligence. The scores that are to be added together to calculate this index are from the following subtests.

Picture Completion Subtest

Block Design Subtest

Matrix Reasoning Subtest

3. The Working Memory Index (WMI)

This index is a measure of working memory and particularly auditory sequential memory. The scores that are to be added together to calculate this index are from the following subtests.

Arithmetic Subtest

Digit Span Subtest

Letter-number sequencing Subtest

4 The Processing Speed Index (PSI)

This test is a measure of both visual sequential memory and the speed of processing visual material. The scores that are to be added together to calculate this index are from the following subtests.

Digit Symbol Coding Subtest

Symbol Search Subtest

The reporting of the four indexes forms a prominent part of the psychological report following the assessment. The four indexes are recorded through the presentation of particular statistics compiled by

analysis of the scored subtests. An explanation of these statistics is presented in the following section.

Understanding the statistics

Reading a psychological report can be a bit daunting at first sight as it often contains the use of statistical terms and statistical phrases that are not in normal everyday use. Some psychologists, in addition to recording the test results, also include statistics relating to the construction of the tests. It is suggested here that the practice of recording statistics other than those relating to the individual's test scores is not necessary in order to understand how dyslexia has been confirmed. Further to this, the reporting of statistics should be kept to a minimum for the ease of interpretation of test results.

Many people are bewildered by statistics. The subject can be a difficult one, especially for people with no interest in mathematics. However, some statistics have to be quoted if the test results are to be made meaningful. It is important, for instance, to know how far the scores obtained are above or below the rest of the population. This information helps to know how severe are the identified weaknesses as well as giving information on the person's level of intelligence.

However, there is no need to study statistics in any real depth in order to understand the basic terms and figures quoted in the

psychologist's report. Moreover, it is not necessary to be able to calculate statistics in order to understand their meaning.

There are only four basic statistical terms that need to be understood when interpreting the psychologist's report on dyslexia. These are 'means', 'standard scores', 'percentiles' and 'index scores'. These are the statistical terms used for recording results in the WAIS III indexes and also in the literacy tests. The four terms are defined below. The explanation of the four statistical terms is simplified for the purposes of non-statisticians. (See Appendix Seven). A fuller interpretations of the terms can be found in statistical handbooks.

The mean score

The mean score refers to an average score. For example, if we consider an individual's score on a test it would be interesting to know where that score stands in comparison with others of the same age. In order to find out, we would look up the score in a table in the test handbook. The table would list mean scores for other people of that particular age. We would find a mean score given alongside other people of the same age of the individual concerned. The mean scores published in the WAIS III have been calculated by adding together thousands of other people's scores and then dividing them by the number of people in the sample.

All of the index scores are based on a mean of 100. The average range on the WAIS III is between 90 and 110. Therefore, any score

below 90 would be considered to be below average. Any score above 110 would be considered to be above average.

Standard or scaled scores

For ease of interpretation, standard scores are also averages obtained from transposing the individual's test scores. The test score is not normally recorded in the psychologist's report. On the WAIS III the scores obtained on each subtest have to be adjusted for age and are these are known as the standard or scaled scores. The standard scores, or scaled scores, on the WAIS III tests each range from 0 to 19. The average standard score for each subtest is 10.

Percentile rank

The WAIS III tests have been standardised on thousands of people of various ages. In the interest of ease of understanding test results percentile rank scores are calculated. These percentile rank scores are based on the results of a hypothetical sample of 100 people.

The percentile rank refers to the number of people who would be expected to score at and above a given percentile. So a percentile score of 95 would mean that if the same test were to be given to 100 people, there would be 95 who would obtain a lower score. By the same token, there would be only 5 who obtain a higher score. As with the mean statistic, the percentiles scores are found in the test

handbook. (Also see Appendix Seven). A percentile statistic and a standard score are usually recorded in the psychological report.

Calculating the index scores

Index scores are calculated by adding together the scaled scores of specific subtests. They have an average range from 90 to 110 as with the traditional Intelligence Quotient.

The following *Table 4.1* illustrates the relationship between standard scores and percentile scores.

Table 4.1 Graphic illustration of the position of standard scores and percentile scores in a normal population

Standard scores	55	70	85	100	115	130	145
Percentiles	1%	2%	16%	50%	84%	98%	99%

The following *Table 4.2* illustrates the percentage of the population expected to score in each category.

Table 4.2 Classification and percentages of index scores

Classification	*Index score*	*% of the population*
Very superior	130 and above	2.2
Superior	120 to 129	6.7
High average	110 to 119	16.1
Average	90 to 109	50.0
Low average	80 to 89	16.1
Borderline	70 to 79	6.7
Extremely low	69 and below	2.2

An example of a person's WAIS III test results might be recorded with indexes and percentiles to look like the following example in *Table 4.3*:

Table 4.3 An example of the recording of WAIS III index scores and percentiles

WAIS III Indexes	Index scores	Percentiles
Verbal Comprehension (VCI)	140	99
Perceptual Organisation (POI)	125	95
Working Memory (WMI)	86	18
Speed of Processing (SPI)	78	7

In the above, *Table 4.3*, there is a marked discrepancy between the two indexes that measure verbal and nonverbal intelligence the VCI and POI and the two that measure Working Memory and Speed of Processing, the WMI and SPI respectively. It would be safe to conclude from this example that the person tested had superior intelligence in verbal intelligence (VCI) and an above average ability in nonverbal intelligence (POI). In contrast to these high scores, their

scores on the remaining two indexes are well below average. This would be considered to be a typical dyslexic profile.

The pattern of results quoted above would confirm dyslexia. The results would suggest that the person would easily understand new material as their intelligence is high. However, the chances are, without appropriate help, they would have difficulty remembering it and also be slow to process it.

Literacy scores

Literacy scores are usually given in terms of reading ages in the case of testing children's reading and spelling. However, reading and spelling ages are not normally calculated when testing adults. Literacy scores with adults are normally recorded in standard or scaled scores. The raw scores are transposed into standard scores at each age level. The average range is 90 to 110. Despite the attempt to avoid age related scores for adults, some students ask for their reading ages and spelling ages. Lecturers and tutors are also known to have requested this information about their students.

The reasons why reading and spelling ages are not normally quoted when testing adults is that by the time children have reached the age of fourteen the majority of them have attained a level of literacy that is at the ceiling of the tests. A reading and spelling age of fourteen would mean that they would be able to read and to spell as well as the average adult. This means that both the average fourteen year old and the average adult would have similar vocabularies and be well able to

read and to spell most available material without difficulty. The average adult would be expected to have the same level of vocabulary and spelling ability as the fourteen year old.

If the same tests were to be given to adults and they scored at the ceiling of the tests as did the fourteen year old, it could be misleading to quote that an adult has a reading age or a spelling age of a fourteen year old. The implication for a person who is not familiar with literacy testing might be that the adult has a mental age of a fourteen year old. This is why the use of standard scores is preferable when testing the reading and spelling of adults.

Interpreting test behaviour

The importance of the psychologist establishing rapport with the person to be tested was discussed in the previous chapter. In the process of establishing rapport with the student, the psychologist would need to be aware of non-cognitive factors described in the previous chapter that could affect the test results. In many cases there would be little of significance to report. However, some people become extremely anxious when under test conditions and this behaviour can affect their test performance. If undue anxiety appeared to have affected the results, the psychological report would contain a separate heading to record this fact. In addition to anxiety affecting test results, self-esteem and locus of control are known major non-cognitive factors that can affect motivation to succeed in the test situation and these would also be recorded.

Summary

Many staff have problems interpreting the psychological report issued following an assessment for dyslexia. This chapter began by discussing the difficulties involved in the interpretation of the psychological report. The recommendation for a national standard and format for reporting the results of the psychological assessment were applauded. The limitations of using the traditional reporting of the intelligence quotient when assessing for possible dyslexia were discussed. The main part of the psychological report usually consists of the recording of the WAIS III test results. However, a simpler, more easily understood method of recording results from the WAIS III was outlined in this chapter.

It is recognised that most people would not be familiar with some of the statistics quoted in the report. It was recommended that there are only four statistical terms that need to be understood and these were explained in this chapter.

The differences between the methods by which literacy tests are recorded in adults and children were discussed in this chapter. In regard to children, the recording of literacy results is usually done in terms of reading and spelling ages. In regard to adults it is preferable

to move away from recording reading and spelling ages. The reasons for this were explained. Finally, in this chapter, reference was made to the need to record non-cognitive factors where they were considered to have influenced the test results.

Chapter 7
How do dyslexic students receive practical support?

Introduction

There are individual techniques and strategies that staff are recommended to use to support dyslexic students but the most support is now provided formally by the particular educational institution. However, the range of support provided varies considerably and depends mainly on the type and size of the educational institution. Some further education colleges and most universities have formal established support services for disabled students and dyslexia is usually included. These support services would normally arrange for the screening procedure for dyslexia a well as arranging the detailed psychological assessment when necessary. Formal support services for dyslexic students are discussed in this chapter.

Unfortunately, many adult educational institutions do not have formal support services for dyslexic students. For many, it would probably be uneconomic to provide a formal service, as for example in a local authority basic educational class. It is particularly important that staff, in that kind of establishment, are aware of how they can support their dyslexic students themselves. Ways in which staff might provide support for their dyslexic students themselves are presented in this chapter.

The most frequently recommended types of technological support available to students with dyslexia are discussed in this chapter. The ways in which tutor/lecturers could support students are also discussed in this chapter. In some cases this could mean adapting their lectures accordingly. In addition to support from the student's educational institution and staff, there are also some common self-help aids that students often find useful. A list of these is given in this chapter. Finally, in this chapter, reference is made to ways in which the students themselves can support each other.

Disability Support Services

Most colleges in further and higher education have an established administrative support service for the support of disabled students, including those with dyslexia. These services make a point of ensuring that students are aware of their existence. The function of a support service is to give general and specific assistance to students with all types of disability, including dyslexia. The support service would also provide general administrative support for those with dyslexia following the psychological assessment. This would normally ensure the implementation of any recommendations made by the professional who confirmed the dyslexia. These recommendations commonly include the provision of technical equipment and perhaps special examination concessions such as extra time or even for the provision of an amanuensis or reader. The support service would also discuss with the student any recommendations that may have been made for a referral to other professionals. For instance, recommendations are often made for the student to receive remedial help in English. A further example would be the overanxious students who might benefit from a referral to a counsellor. The institutions support services would normally arrange for these referrals.

In higher education, the psychological assessment is usually followed up by what is known as a 'needs assessment' interview with a professional from the support service. Further recommendations may be made at this interview but the main aim of the needs assessment is to discuss with the student details of the recommended technical equipment and how to obtain it.

Support services sometimes exist independently but most are organised as part of a student welfare advisory service. Some may also form part of a college student counselling service. Some support services employ a dyslexia-trained tutor who conducts individual testing for students and who also may organise a college screening programme for dyslexic students. Where the tutor/lecturer also has an appropriate qualification in the testing of dyslexia they may also be asked to conduct the detailed psychological assessment when the screening procedure has revealed symptoms of dyslexia. This practice is probably going to increase in the coming years as more teachers are encouraged to undertake the specialist training in dyslexia assessment. A national association of specialists in the assessment of dyslexia has recently been established in the UK for people working in the higher education sector and one of their aims is to ensure that there is proper provision for dyslexic students in all higher education establishments.

The more far-thinking institutions have 'dyslexia awareness' programmes. A major aim of most of these services is to help students and staff to raise their awareness of dyslexia. Many services organise staff development courses on the topic of supporting students with dyslexia.

A major function of the support service is to administer the recommendations listed in the psychological report. Many of the recommendations will involve not only the provision for the student of special equipment but also the purchase of time from other professionals. The financing of other professionals recommended in the psychological report would also be administered by the student support service.

Whatever the form of the student support service, the student with dyslexia in higher education would be well advised to consult with this service early in their college career.

The Disability Support Allowance in Higher Education

An important function of college support service in higher education would be to send a copy of the psychological report with its recommendations to the Local Education Authority (LEA). This is because students in higher education are eligible to receive a disability allowance from their LEA for the purchase of recommended equipment. It is something of an anomaly that at present students in other educational establishments such as those students in further education are not eligible to receive this grant. There is provision however, for FE Colleges to apply for additional funding for dyslexic students through the Learning Skills Council.

Where the student is eligible the local education authority normally provides funding for the purchase of equipment that may have been recommended in the psychological report. Although the funding is mainly used for the purchase of technical equipment, it can also be used for the purchase of other types of support recommended, such as financing professional time for such as remedial help or counselling. The support service usually offers guidance to the student on this procedure. The funding is known as the Disability Support Allowance (DSA). Provided the LEA is satisfied that the report contains sufficient evidence for dyslexia and is assured that the author of the report is properly qualified to have administered the assessment there is usually no problem in the student receiving the allowance.

All dyslexic students on approved courses in higher education are eligible to apply for the DSA. Part-time students who take at least 50% of a course are also eligible. It is hoped that in the not too distant future students in further education and those in basic adult education classes would also be eligible to receive this grant.

Recommendations in the psychological report

Once dyslexia has been confirmed in a student, the professional who conducted the assessment procedure would normally issue a report as described in Chapter 6. An important part of this report should outline appropriate practical recommendations for supporting the student in their studies. These recommendations usually include details of how best the student can be helped to compensate for the identified weaknesses. For example, if slowness in reading has been identified the psychologist would recommend extra time for the student in examinations. Extra time recommended varies according to the severity of the condition but on average an extra twenty minutes per hour of examination time would be recommended. Other recommendations often include specific suggestions for the purchase of special equipment by the student such as computers and dictaphones. Reports may also contain recommendations for engaging outside help from other professionals. Examples of these would be a referral to a remedial service to enhance literacy skills, a referral to a counsellor where emotional problems have been identified and perhaps a referral to the appropriate professional for an assessment of possible scotopic sensitivity. Recommendations are usually tailored to the individual needs of the student as identified in the psychological assessment.

Lecturer and tutor support

Tutors and lecturers have an important part to play in supporting their dyslexic students whether or not their educational institution has a formal support centre. This support comes naturally to most tutors and lecturers once they have been made aware of the difficulties faced by their students with dyslexia. Sometimes lecturers and tutors may be asked to amend their approach to their teaching in the light of the recommendations made following the psychological assessment. For instance, they may be asked to provide more handouts to students and to use more visual aids. Appropriate handouts are a must for most students with weaknesses in working memory as copying from an overhead projector is often slow.

Students with dyslexia vary in the kind of difficulties they experience but most will have difficulties with the processing of information that is presented both visually and orally. Accordingly, the lecturer will need to give especial consideration to how they present their course material ensuring where possible that it compensates for their dyslexic students' specific weaknesses. They may for instance need to supplement their lecture with appropriate handouts, often of a visual kind.

Staff in further education and those in basic education classes who are involved in the teaching of basic educational skills tend to identify possible dyslexic students very quickly as obviously their main focus is on literacy. In the field of higher education, the dyslexic student's difficulties are not always so quickly discovered. Quite often their dyslexia may not become apparent until they have submitted some written work. Their symptoms may also be revealed in their performance in discussion groups where they may be slow to respond as word retrieval is often slow for those with dyslexia. As lecturers and tutors are in frequent contact with students they are often the first to identify the student with dyslexia.

The student support services in higher education normally will have given lecturers the names of students who have been diagnosed with dyslexia. Even with such a procedure in place, it would be wise for the student to introduce themselves to their lecturers at the beginning of the course. However, in practice this does not always happen. Some students may be reluctant to approach their lecturers. There are various reasons for this, the most common reason being reluctance to appear to be obtaining an unfair advantage over student colleagues. They may also have feelings of inadequacy over their dyslexia and misguidedly try to cope without concessions. Tutors/lectures should therefore attempt to contact those students with dyslexia who have not made themselves known to them early in the course.

On receiving the psychological report, most lecturers and tutors are usually only too ready to comply with the recommendations made and to accommodate the needs of dyslexic students. In isolated cases, this may prove to be difficult for the lecturer but a compromise solution can usually be agreed upon after discussion with the student and/or the college's support services.

On first being informed that they are dyslexic, some students experience acute anxieties and need to talk about this. Their tutor or lecturer is often the person they relate to best. Consequently, tutors/lecturers should be prepared for this and try to provide time for the students.

In a seminar group it is often helpful if the lecturer deliberately turns to the student with dyslexia and asks them for a comment as the more talkative members of the group can dominate them. In large groups it is often too intimidating for dyslexic students to respond orally and they should not be expected to do so.

Students with dyslexia are also often slow to process incoming information, especially oral information. An analogy would be to liken their brain to a tape recorder with a short loop. The memory part of the brain is quickly overloaded just as in a tape recorder with a short loop. They are often unable to do anything with the new information without, in effect, making more room on the loop by 'wiping off' the earlier information. Lecturers should therefore give oral instructions sparingly and be prepared to have to repeat them.

All new subjects contain new words and new concepts. As students with dyslexia will have particular difficulty remembering new words, particular attention should be drawn to any new words. They should be highlighted visually as well as emphasised during the lecture and students encouraged to associate the new material with earlier learned material already stored in their long-term memory.

Dyslexic students tend to be sensitive about their learning difficulty and tutors/lectures should be prepared for an occasional emotional outburst without overreacting to it. This possible problem is discussed in more detail in the following chapter.

Practical and technological support

The computer

Most dyslexic students have a problem with organizing their written work, so a computer or word processor can be of considerable benefit to them. Most students diagnosed as being dyslexic will have a weakness in short-term memory and in one sense a computer could be considered to be their memory. There are numerous benefits to be had using a computer or word processor.

Students with dyslexia will usually be slow to process most kinds of information. Writing essays can be unusually slow as word retrieval is often difficult. It is not uncommon to hear a dyslexic student assert, 'The words are on the tip of my tongue. I know what I want to say but I can't just get the right words.' The thesaurus on a computer programme is of great benefit in such circumstances.

A computer will not only speed up their work but its spellchecker will also help with spelling. Spelling is often a problem for students with dyslexia. It can be particularly satisfying for students when they are able to correct spelling mistakes without having to look up the words in a dictionary and then perhaps having to erase them. Also, nobody else but the student will have seen the original mistakes made so the resultant presentation of the work will be immediately acceptable. To see the finished article in correct and neat form can be a great morale booster for a student who in the past has had to submit work with an untidy appearance.

Those with grammar weaknesses will also benefit from an appropriate computer programme. As with spelling, the computer programme will identify any errors and where grammatical errors are made whole sentences and paragraphs can be moved around in seconds. Again, this can be done without leaving a trace of the original errors.

Many students with dyslexia have some degree of confused laterality. They may not only be slow to select left and right but also they can have trouble with the order of words and even with the order of sentences. Again, the computer programmes can help here.

When students are anxious about their performance, handwriting can be untidy and in extreme case it can be unintelligible. Careful concentration on remedying this can mean that the student is unusually slow to write. Not having to use a pen is a boon to such a student. It is of particular benefit to those with dyspraxia who may have a fine motor coordination weakness. Even the manipulation of a keyboard can be a difficult maneuver for some students, again, especially those with dyspraxia. In such cases a voice-activated computer would be recommended to obviate the need to have to manipulate the keyboard.

There are various pieces of computer software for dyslexic students that provide suitable help when writing essays. One example of these programmes that is becoming popular for dyslexic students, is one known as *Read and Write*. This programme provides speech feedback and contains a phonetic spellchecker. It also contains a talking calculator.

The Reading Pen

Sometimes students may not have immediate access to a computer and have to use a pen. There is a recent electronic invention for these occasions that enables students with spelling difficulties to receive immediate feedback on any words miss-spelt. If a word is miss-spelt while writing, the word appears in a small window at the side of the pen. If the writing is continued the pen then supplies the correct version of the word. There is also a version of the pen that produces definitions and pronunciations. Use of the pen requires adequate hand-eye dexterity so it would not be suitable for use by those with dyspraxia.

A Scanner

Students with dyslexia find that the borrowing of library books is usually a problem owing to their slowness in processing information. The use of a scanner is one way of getting around the problem. A scanner enables students to copy various pages from library books and other material and then put them into their computers. This should always be done of course within the legal requirements for photocopying material that may be copyright.

A Dictaphone

Note-taking is a problem for those students with an auditory memory weakness so permission to tape record lectures is often recommended in the psychologist's report.

A weakness in auditory sequential memory is a common problem for dyslexic students. As a result of this difficulty, taking notes in lectures is always difficult. A recommendation for permission to tape record lectures would obviate the need to take down notes. The lecture can then be listened to without the added strain of having also to write it down. It would then be played back later at leisure.

Electronic Spellcheckers

Most students with dyslexia have some problems with spelling. A word-processor with a spellchecker is a boon for many when working at home. When needing to spell correctly in college, or away from the computer, a handheld spellchecker is equally useful. There are several on the market that can identify misspelled words and then correct them. Most of them will also have a thesaurus component. This is particularly useful for students who find word retrieval a problem. Some colleges will also allow these handheld spellcheckers into an examination.

Training in the use of technology

Not all students are familiar with the use of a computer or with these new electronic inventions. In such cases a recommendation for training in their use is usually made. Most institutions run courses on using computers and word processors and introduce the student to the different soft ware packages available that can further benefit those with dyslexia.

Support in examinations

Extra time

Speed of processing material is generally slow for students diagnosed as being dyslexic. Even if they are able to keep a reasonable writing speed they often need extra time to reread their work to ensure correct grammar and spelling. This is why extra time in examinations is often recommended for these students. The amount of extra time recommended will depend on the severity of the dyslexia. Extra time can range from ten minutes to thirty minutes in every one hour of examination time for a student who has been diagnosed as being dyslexic.

Provision for an amanuensis

For some students, their dyslexia is so severe that even the granting of extra time in an examination does not help. For these students a recommendation for the provision of an amanuensis, or reader, is often made. Poor fine motor coordination skills may make their written work unintelligible. More commonly, their weak working memory can cause them to take an inordinate amount of time to read and /or to write even the shortest of essays.

Also, there are those students whose reading and spelling attainments may be so weak that even if given extra time they still struggle to write legibly. These students probably have to spend time reading and rereading over again both the examination questions and their work in order to check and to correct their mistakes.

Private room

Most people experience a degree of anxiety when having to sit a public examination. For some, however, the anxiety can be so severe as to be incapacitating. This is usually the case where the person concerned has disabilities that may interfere with their performance. The person with dyslexia is a common example of this. It is known that undue anxiety can prevent clear thinking so it is essential that students with dyslexia be helped to remain calm during examinations. Relaxation techniques can be learned prior to the examination. These are discussed in the following chapter.

Where a student is subject to acute anxiety the psychological assessment will usually have identified it and recommended help for it. In addition to helping the anxious student through the learning of appropriate relaxation techniques, special examination arrangements can be made. Permission can be given for anxious students to sit the examination privately in a separate room. In rare cases, anxiety can make the act of writing impossible. For those students permission would have to be sought for them to be examined orally or perhaps through dictating their answers into a tape recorder.

Study skills assistance

Students whose reading and/or spelling are particularly weak may benefit from one-to-one tuition in literacy skills. Many of these students would be the students for whom an amanuensis has been recommended in examinations. The research evidence would say that most adults with dyslexia are going to have some difficulty with spelling. However, the research would indicate that literacy skills could usually be improved to some degree with appropriate remedial help.

Other study skills assistance

There are also other kinds of help that can be obtained under this umbrella of Study Skills Assistance. One example is guidance in essay writing. The construction of essays is often difficult for those with dyslexia. Many students, who may have excellent creative ideas often have a problem when it comes to ordering their ideas and using the correct grammar. There is a tendency for students with dyslexia to ramble on when not familiar with common grammatical forms. Providing someone to proof read the student's work before it is formally submitted can make a tremendous difference. The difference is not only seen in a more polished product but also in the student's morale.

Self-help aids

While there are many avenues of support for students with dyslexia, as listed above, there are many other ways in which students can support themselves. There are several strategies that students can learn in order to compensate for their weaknesses. Some of these are so successful that with practice the student can soon mask the dyslexia completely.

Having to recall long lists of numbers can present problems to students both in their academic work and socially. Remembering telephone numbers is a common problem. A recommended method of remembering this is first to break down the numbers into smaller units. So instead of trying to remember the sequence, 8, 6, 9, 1, 5, 2, this list of six units could be broken down into only three units as follows: 86, 91, 52. Only three numbers have to be remembered rather than six numbers.

Using mnemonics

This memory aid is a popular one for the learning of most kinds of facts. It is far best if students devise their own mnemonics. The following example is given for those who may not be familiar with this technique. The mnemonic is STAR. This is one the author devised several years ago for people who had panic attacks.

S…stop

T...talk to yourself

A...action

R...relaxation

The principle behind the mnemonic is association of ideas. When one idea is recalled it will tend to awaken other related ideas. (See further explanation of the use of STAR in Chapter 9).

Reinforcing the verbal message with the visual message

Whenever a verbal instruction is received it always helps to be able to visualise it as well as to hear it. For instance, if driving and an instruction given to turn either to the left or to the right it helps to have the letters L and R displayed prominently in front of the driver. The visual one would then reinforce the verbal message.

The ability to distinguish left from right is a very common difficulty amongst children diagnosed with dyslexia. By adulthood people have usually learned their left from their right. However, there is still often a delay in responding. In these cases a memory aid does help for a quicker response.

The making of lists is always useful, especially when shopping. Once again, it is the visual image that reinforces the idea.

The value of reinforcing verbal messages or an idea with a visual message is based on the well-known principle known as conditioning. Conditioning illustrates the phenomenon that if one piece of behaviour is regularly paired with another different kind of behaviour, the appearance of one of them will immediately recall the other one. So whenever we say "fish" there is a tendency to think "chips". This principle can be used for remembering a multitude of facts. For instance, finding it hard to remember a person's name it should be paired with something else that is novel, e.g. if the person's name is "Green" it might be helpful to associate it with "grass".

Organising the day

Keeping appointments and remembering appointment times is usually a problem for the dyslexic. A diary is essential for this purpose. The nature of the appointment, the day and the time should all be entered into the diary as soon as the appointments are made. Many students will find that a whiteboard is more useful than a pocket diary for ensuring they do not forget appointments. This is because they are able to see the information immediately in front of them and also see it in relation to other tasks of the day that they may also have to accomplish.

Overlearning

Any material that has to be memorized can present problems when having to recall it. Students are often perplexed when they forget a piece of work that they felt that they had learned well. The learning of a piece of poetry would be an example of this. The usual attempt to memorise a poem involves repeating it until it can be recited from memory. However, it is essential for the student who is dyslexic that they over-learn this kind of material. This means not being satisfied with only one, or even two, correct recitations of the material. It is necessary to continue to recite the passage for several more recitations, after the first correct one. There is research evidence to show that this method of over-learning material results in being able to retain the information much longer.

Forming a student support group

Some students benefit from being members of a support group comprising other students diagnosed with dyslexia. This kind of support can be very effective in reducing feelings of isolation that many students experience on first being diagnosed with dyslexia. Students are often amazed and also comforted to know just how many others students in their college has similar problems. The organisation of such a group will depend largely the number of students involved but they are usually small enough to be sufficiently informal for intimate discussions of their dyslexia. The group may be a social group only but it could be encouraged to develop into a learning support group also. Proof reading one another's work and self-checking of assignments could be incorporated into the group's programme of activities. Finally, the more formally organised of these support groups might occasionally like to invite outside speakers to their meetings. Useful contacts for this purpose can be found at the offices of the British Dyslexia Association and/or the Adult Dyslexia Organisation. (Addresses for these are given in Appendix Three.)

Summary

The many ways in which the student with dyslexia can receive general and practical support have been discussed in this chapter. Most support can come from a formally established college disability support service. The usual functions of a support service were outlined.

The various recommendations for supporting dyslexic students outlined in the psychological report were discussed. The role of the tutors and lecturers in implementing some of these recommendations was also discussed.

The types of support that were discussed in this chapter fall into three categories. Firstly, there is the kind of support recommended in the psychological report and normally administered by the student support services in the college. Secondly, there is the kind of support provided by tutors and lecturers. Thirdly, there is self-help support.

Students can be encouraged to conduct their own self-help. Ways in which they might do this were outlined. Self-help also includes the possible formation of mutual support groups comprising other students with dyslexia.

The ways in which tutors and lecturers might meet the emotional needs of their students with dyslexia are discussed in the next two chapters.

Chapter 8
Why do some dyslexic students have a problem coping with the diagnosis of dyslexia?

Introduction

Most students with dyslexia seem to cope well emotionally and with proper support they succeed with their chosen course of studies. However, many students have difficulty coping with the knowledge that they are dyslexic and welcome an opportunity to discuss this. Moreover, talking about how they felt when diagnosed as being dyslexic is often a problem for dyslexic students. Communication generally is a common source of frustration for people with dyslexia, whether in the written mode or the oral mode. People with dyslexia may know what they want to say or want to write but often the correct words are slow to appear. The correct words may evade them altogether. This kind of frustration can result in low self-esteem as well as producing anxieties.

Many students have a problem coming to terms with their dyslexia. However, not all students with dyslexia react in the same way. Some students appear to over react, while others, in contrast, seem to be relatively unaffected. This chapter begins by exploring basic personality types that are responsible for the different ways in which dyslexic students react to their dyslexia. The more that these differences are understood the better the chances of communication. Knowledge of basic personality factors can be the first step in improving communication. Also, an understanding of personality differences usually helps to establish a more positive attitude when communicating.

As referred to earlier, dyslexia can cause many frustrations for adult students. As a result of their language difficulties, students with dyslexia often manifest behavior that is misinterpreted. They can easily give a false impression of being negative towards another person when in fact their behaviour is more likely to be directed towards themselves. This frustrates them even further. Knowledge of the common reactions to frustration together with information on basic personality differences can often help the tutor/lecturer understand and clarify this behaviour. The common reactions to frustration are discussed in this chapter.

Communication is a two-way process and it is important that accurate verbal messages are used. As an aid to this, a well researched model of communication using the correct verbal messages will be outlined in this chapter.

Finally, in this chapter, a list of desirable personal qualities conducive to improved communication that can be developed in both the students and the tutor or lecturer will be discussed.

Basic Personality Differences

It is a truism to assert that everybody is different. Personality is unique. No two people are exactly alike; even identical twins have subtle differences in personality. While there is ample research evidence to show that heredity plays a large part in producing these differences, there is evidence that environmental factors also play a part. The question to be asked is what proportion of differences in personality is due to heredity and what proportion is due to environment?

This question has intrigued philosophers for centuries. In more recent times, it has also been a topic of debate and research for psychologists. In order to answer the relative influences of heredity and environment in more precise terms psychologists have devised methods of measuring personality traits. One of the leading pioneers in this field was Hans Eysenck (1977). Eysenck and his associates devised questionnaires and gave them to thousands of people at all age levels, including identical twins.

Following a sophisticated method of statistical analysis of the questionnaire results, they concluded that there are only two

dimensions of personality that are likely to be inherited. He provided evidence that all other personality traits are learned. The personality traits that he claimed to be inherited can be measured along two dimensions. These are:

Introversion/extraversion; and Neuroticism (emotionality). Eysenck concluded that people can be measured along both these dimensions. Moreover, the continuum would follow the normal curve of distribution, i.e., most people are in the middle of the dimension with only a few at either end of it. So in practice most people are found to be a mixture of introversion and extraversion.

Introversion/extraversion

It is a fact of life that there some people who prefer quiet pursuits and are usually relatively quiet in the company of others. By the same token, there are other people who prefer noisy pursuits and are usually described as being 'the life and soul of the party' when at a social gathering. The first group would be referred to as introverted and the second group referred to as extraverted. The work of Eysenck revealed that there is likely to be a physiological basis for this difference. The results of electrographic tests (EEG) measuring a person's electrical impulses in the brain, show marked differences between the two groups. The alpha and beta wave patterns of the introverted group were seen to be high in amplitude and closer together. The same wave patterns in the extraverted group were seen to be low in amplitude and spaced wider apart. The significance of

these differences is that those alpha and beta waves that are high in amplitude indicate that the cortex in the brain is being over-stimulated while the opposite is true of the wave patterns that are seen to be low in amplitude. On the principle of homeostasis, meaning that nature requires a balance in all things, those people whose cortex is over-stimulated will be quieter than those people whose cortex appears to be under-stimulated. The former group has enough stimulation in contrast to the latter group that probably craves more stimulation. The more extraverted group would generally seek excitement, preferably in the company of lots of other people. In contrast to this group, the more introverted group would perhaps prefer to read a book alone or seek the company of only one or two other people.

Neuroticism (Emotionality)

Emotionality refers to the extent to which people experience emotions and is based on a person's physiological makeup. The autonomic nervous system, responsible for expression of emotions, reacts differently in different people. As with the introvert/extravert dimension, most people are in the middle of a continuum. People at one end of this continuum would be relatively unemotional while those at the opposite end of the continuum would have a tendency to be over-emotional. The first group when happy would be elated and when unhappy they would be in the depths of depression.

It can be appreciated that when frustrated the highly emotional person is their own worst enemy. Their emotions can swamp them and when this happens they cannot think clearly. There is research evidence showing that too much emotion interferes with both thinking and memory functions.

It would not be unreasonable to believe that to be unemotional is the desired state. However, there is research evidence here to show that some emotion is necessary for learning to take place. It seems that both too much and too little emotion are both undesirable states in relation to learning. There is an optimum level of emotion necessary for any learning task. The problem is in finding how much would be desirable for any individual task. There is some evidence that arts subjects require more emotion than science subjects but overall the evidence for this scanty. There are so many other factors that contribute to achievement and have to be taken into consideration.

Common reactions to frustration

There are several sources of potential frustration for dyslexic students in adult education. There is little doubt, however, that a common source of frustration is being unable to express themselves easily. People generally vary in the way they express their frustration. The ways in which this frustration is manifested depends largely on a person's personality make up. Different personality types tend to react in terms of their personality type. The more extraverted person would

react outwardly to frustration while the more introverted type would react inwardly to the same source of frustration. A dyslexic extraverted student who is frustrated might easily shout and may even attack the source of frustration. A more introverted dyslexic student would be more inclined to suffer in silence. If the person is also highly emotional the effects of the frustration are even more keenly felt.

Either way, when frustrated in this way most people will instinctively show behaviour that is designed to protect their self-esteem. Particular defense mechanisms are adopted that are sometimes even outside a person's level of consciousness. In other words, they are often unaware that they are employing them. It is useful for tutors and lecturers to be prepared for these.

Denial

This means a refusal to accept any inferiority. There is a tendency for denial to take place whenever an experience is too painful to be acknowledged. An example of this would be a dyslexic student who cannot accept that they have a weak short-term memory and so need to write down any instructions given by their lecturer.

Blaming others

Students with dyslexia often are slower to process information than other students and it is hard for some of them to accept this. This type of student may sometimes subconsciously blame other people for their slow progress.

Rationalisation

This means giving a 'face-saving' reason for a perceived failure. Having to complete assignments within particular time constraints is not easy for many adult dyslexics. Failure to meet a deadline in this way is more bearable if they can offer an excuse such as they were ill at the time.

Compensation

This refers to a person's attempt to compensate for an inferiority feeling by focusing on excelling in some other field. It can also refer to the adoption of a compensatory attitude. An example of this would be when a person who feels inadequate because of their small size develops a loud voice. A person who regularly demonstrates this kind of behaviour is often referred to as having an inferiority complex.

The Gordon model

The work of Thomas Gordon (1974) in techniques of classroom communication is generally recognised as being a classic in the field of self-esteem enhancement. Gordon shows how it is possible by the judicious use of the right words to enhance self-esteem when talking to children. He also shows how it is possible to reduce self-esteem by using the wrong words. The main tenets of Gordon's work apply equally to adults as well as to children and are advocated for

tutors/lecturers when talking to adult students. It is especially advocated in those unfortunate circumstances when a tutor/lecturer may have to discipline a student. It is too easy to reduce a student's self-esteem and to lose their cooperation completely if the wrong words are used.

The main principle of Gordon's Model is the formula 'I- when-because'. Most of us, when feeling irritated or aggressive, will end to use the word 'you'. Let us suppose that a lecturer has to complain to a student over regular late coming without ever an apology being offered by the student. The lecturer might say the following: 'you are being a nuisance coming late every lesson'. This is referred to as using a 'you' message. However, if the Gordon Model had been used the lecturer would have used different words. This time the lecturer would have used the words 'I, when, because' and said instead, 'I feel angry when you come late because it inconveniences other students when I have to go over work twice.'

The reasons for using these three words are as follows:

'*I*' – This word allows the lecturers to express their feelings about the behaviour and thus helps to reduce their frustration.

'*When*' – The use of this word describes the offending behaviour and implies that the complaint is not global. It is in reference to a specific situation only, so giving the student an opportunity to reform.

'*Because*' – This word gives a reason for the complaint and so shows that the complaint is not merely a whim of the lecturer.

Using this Model of communication is considered to be using an assertive response rather than an aggressive one. The following two dramatic scenes illustrate this Model further.

Scene 1

Lecturer You are always late for this lecture. Why are you such a nuisance?

Student I am not always late and I don't like being called a nuisance.

Lecturer But you are a nuisance. Just ask the other students.

Student I don't think you are being fair. I don't think I'll come here again.

Lecturer Please yourself. There'll be other students who do want to come.

Main Points of Scene 1

The lecturer was using ‘You’ messages, and so tending to lower self-esteem.

It was interpreted as an attack on the student’s integrity.

The lecturer’s first comment was bound to provoke an aggressive reply from the student.

The lecturer’s comments were bound to reduce self-esteem through public humiliation.

There was no opportunity for the student to offer to reform.

A wholly negative atmosphere was created throughout the encounter.

Scene 2

Lecturer I am disappointed when you always come late for this lecture.

Student Sorry, I had to call in the shop on the way for my lunch. Why does it matter?

Lecturer The main reason is that when I have to repeat some of the lecture it inconveniences other students.’

Student Sorry I’ll try to be on time for the next lecture

Lecturer OK.

Main points of scene 2

’I’ messages were being used so the initial focus was on the lecturer’s feelings.

By using 'when' the implication was that it was only this piece of behaviour that was the object of complaint and not the student's whole personality.

Self-esteem was not threatened so it did not result in an aggressive reply.

By using 'because' it implied that the complaint was reasonable.

A positive atmosphere for possible reform by the student was established.

Non-verbal cues

Whenever two people engage in a conversation their communication contains not only verbal messages but also non-verbal messages. The work of Michael Argyle (1997) shows how people are often more aware of non-verbal behaviour than verbal messages. It has been shown how students at a lecture often forget the contents of the lecture but will always remember the lecturer's appearance and what the lecturer sounded like. Amongst typical non-verbal behaviour would be voice tone, facial expressions, hand gestures and body posture.

It seems that non-verbal behaviour is instinctive and more accurately reflects a person's true feelings. While it is possible to lie about feelings using appropriate verbal messages it is not so easy to disguise non-verbal behaviour. Ideally, a person's verbal and their non-verbal would be synchronized in conversation.

Achieving congruence between verbal and non-verbal communication

The Gordon Model described above assumes that the lecturer's non-verbal behaviour is synchronized with the lecturer's verbal

behaviour. This also assumes that the lecturer in question is genuinely concerned to help the student reform. The personal quality of being genuine is a personality characteristic identified by Carl Rogers (1967) as an essential quality for a counsellor. Rogers also identified the personal qualities of acceptance and empathy as being essential characteristics in a successful counsellor. Further research led Rogers to the conclusion that people who have these three qualities communicate best. It is not intended to suggest that tutors and lecturers should be counsellors although some may well act in this role from time to time. What is advocated is that in the interests of communicating with their students, tutors and lecturers should become familiar with the three desirable qualities of personality identified by Rogers. These qualities are explained below.

Genuineness

People who are genuine are able to 'be themselves'. They are usually able to express their true feelings and their opinions to others. Many people however, are inhibited in this respect and are unable to say what they really mean. Sometimes this is done out of sympathy or respect for another's point of view. Unfortunately, there are some people who seem unable to be themselves no matter what the circumstances and tend to hide behind a public persona. When this happens it is difficult to know what these people are really thinking on any topic. Obviously, this would interfere with communication as they would not be easily trusted. Moreover, if this kind of behaviour is taken to extreme, there is evidence that to be always completely and

totally false is bad for a person's mental health. With regard to communicating with students, tutors and lecturers who are genuine will discover that they soon obtain the trust of their students.

Acceptance

This quality refers to the ability to respect a person even if their behaviour is not worthy of respect. It requires an ability to see the person behind the behaviour and is a quality that is not easily learned. It is more of a philosophy of basic respect for human dignity than a technique and is usually communicated nonverbally. People who have a genuine respect for others are accepting of them and this will be reflected through their non-judgemental behaviour. Children are particularly adept at knowing whether an adult is accepting or not. This might be because adults generally tend to be less aware of body language. Even so, if a person does not like another it usually shows in their body language.

Empathy

This quality means being able to experience what another person is feeling and to be able to communicate this to the other person. It is a quality that can be developed with practice. It requires the ability to be able to 'listen' to another's feelings as well as to the content of their words. This can be accomplished by focusing on the emotionality of what they are saying and on their body language while they are talking. Once the other person's feelings have been identified it is important that they 'feed' back to the other person that they appreciate

their feelings. The following two dramatic scenes illustrate the quality of empathy. Scene one is without empathy and scene two is with empathy.

Scene 1

Student	(With anxious face). Could I please have a word with you about my assignment?
Lecturer	Sure. How about in my room tomorrow morning at 10am?
Student	(Hesitating). Well, I wondered if I might talk to you now.
Lecturer	Sorry, can't it wait? What's the problem? I have some shopping to do.
Student	(Quietly). I suppose it will have to wait..
Lecturer	See you tomorrow then. Goodbye until then.

Student (With grim expression). OK.

Scene 2 *(with empathy)*

Student (With anxious face) Could I please have a word with you about my assignment?

Lecturer Sure. You sound a bit worried. I have to do some shopping but that could wait.

Student (Worried expression). You are right. I am a bit worried. I don't think I'll be able to do it.

Lecturer Oh, why is that?

Student I just cannot understand the question.

Lecturer Would you like to talk about it now?

Student (Brightening up) Yes, that would be good.

In scene 1, the lecturer did not appreciate how worried was the student. There was no empathy. In scene 2, the lecturer saw the student's facial expression and appreciated the student's anxious feelings. The deduced feelings were then reflected back to the student. This provided confirmation of the feelings and also communicated that the student was being understood. Communication was thus enhanced. The student felt that a psychological bridge had been built between them. The student then felt sufficiently comfortable to reveal the source of concern.

The Modelling Effect

When communication is at its best we sometimes say that people are 'on the same wavelength'. They appear to understand and to trust each other. They feel safe to communicate without being anxious over possible criticism. The lecturer or tutor who has been able to establish this kind of communication with a student is privileged, as dyslexic students are often sensitive to criticism. They have usually experienced plenty of it in life generally while coping with their dyslexia. Those students whose dyslexia was not identified until they entered adult education probably experienced criticism also during their early education.

The tutor/lecturer who is empathetic, accepting, genuine and who also has learned how to maintain the self-esteem of the student as described above, will provide a powerful model for students. The modelling effect has been the subject of much research since the early work of Bandura (1970). Once this effect takes place the tutor/lecturer can have a very positive influence on a student's progress. Many adult students find it hard to resume formal education especially where there has been a prolonged gap since their school days. Through the modeling effect, tutors/lecturers can often provide students with the necessary impetus and motivation to persevere with their studies.

Summary

This chapter set out first to help dyslexic students and professional staff to understand why many dyslexic students have a problem communicating their feelings about their dyslexia. Many students do appear to be over sensitive to their dyslexia and may react to it in ways that can be disturbing. People with dyslexia are at risk of developing psychological problems unless their dyslexia is handled wisely. The communication skills of the staff dealing with the students are crucial in handling this kind of problem. The second half of this chapter focused on helping students and tutor/lecturers develop their communication skills and in so doing help students come to terms with their feelings about their dyslexia.

The first step in developing these skills is to be aware of the reason for personality differences. The Eysenck personality types and their meanings were outlined showing how there appears to be two major personality dimensions that are inherited.

Using the correct words when communicating was also emphasised and the Gordon Model of communication was recommended for use in this respect. The work of Carl Rogers in identifying desirable qualities of personality that will enhance communication was cited as an example of the recommended approach for tutors/lecturers. These qualities of acceptance, genuineness and empathy were discussed in order to achieve congruence of both verbal and non-verbal behaviour. Dramatic scenes illustrating the main points of both the Gordon model and the communication work of Carl Rogers were presented.

The chapter concluded with reference to the Modelling Effect, first noted by Bandura. This was cited as an example of the positive influence that tutors/lecturers can have on students once effective communication has been established.

Chapter 9
How can dyslexic students receive emotional support?

Introduction.

Recent research indicates that dyslexic students in Higher Education show more anxiety than students without any learning difficulties (Carroll and Iles, 2006). Moreover, this anxiety is not merely evident in relation to their studies but is also present in many social situations. A tutor or lecturer is often the first person to become aware of this anxiety and of their students' general emotional needs. Some students clearly have emotional needs that require expert help and would need to be referred to an appropriate specialist. There are some students with less severe emotional needs that could often be resolved by a sensitive staff member without resorting to an outside referral. An often asked question by staff is whether they are able themselves to help this type of student or whether they should always seek expert help. This depends on the severity of the student's emotional state. Some tutors and lecturers establish such a trusting relationship with their students that they find that their students sometimes come to them spontaneously for emotional support. It is not suggested that these staff adopt a formal counselling role but they are often in the best position to know when a student is in distress and

there are strategies they can provide to give the students the necessary support. Some of these strategies are self-help programmes that tutors and lectures might wish to introduce to their students. These strategies and programmes are outlined in this chapter.

Amongst the milder emotional difficulties often presented by students is a degree of anxiety with reading, writing and spelling as a result of being identified as being dyslexic at school or even later at college. They remember the feelings of embarrassment and anxiety they experienced when learning to read and spell during their school days. Although most adult students eventually learn the skills of reading and writing the negative emotions associated with their initial learning of the skills often remain. Tutors and lecturers need to know how best to manage this kind of behaviour if a student presents them with this kind of problem. Practical methods of coping with this kind of anxiety are discussed in this chapter.

Students with learning difficulties are always at risk of developing low self-esteem (Lawrence, 2006). Of particular significance is the research evidence showing an association between difficulties in literacy skills and self-esteem. Research into the development of self-esteem has continually shown a positive correlation between levels of self-esteem and literacy skills. The chances are that many dyslexic students in adult education will have developed low self-esteem during their school days and this will have persisted.

This chapter outlines ways in which students can be helped to overcome negative emotions associated with previous failure experiences and so reduce their anxiety levels. A particular strategy is outlined also to help students to reduce their own anxiety with a self-help programme. It has been devised by the author (Lawrence, 2000) and is based upon the well-known method of treatment for emotional difficulties, known as Cognitive Behavioural Therapy. The chapter also includes a self-help programme showing students how to enhance their self-esteem.

The chapter also outlines how lecturers and tutors can provide a learning environment conducive to the enhancement of self-esteem. The need for more intensive counselling for some students is also discussed.

The first type of emotional support that most students with dyslexia need is for reassurance regarding the labels of disabled and dyslexia. This chapter begins by discussing some students' emotional reactions to these labels.

Reassurance regarding the labels dyslexia and disabled

It is not easy for some students to accept that they have been diagnosed with dyslexia. In fact, many students say that they hope they will be able to keep their dyslexia quiet. Perhaps this is understandable when they know now that dyslexia is an official

category of disability. It would appear that it is the word disabled that upsets them the most. All words have emotional connotations and sometimes students can become particularly upset when confronted for the first time with the label of disability. The student needs to be reassured first that the label 'disability' is not meant to imply that they are disabled in the medical sense and that the word disability is a purely administrative label. It seems that it is the fact that the specific learning difficulty known as dyslexia is on the same list of recognised disabilities such as sensory disorders, neurological impairments and various physical disabilities that concerns many students. It is worth communicating to the student showing concern that The British Medical Association also had trouble accepting dyslexia as a disability when in the 1970s it issued an official statement that 'dyslexia is not a medical condition but an educational one'. Since this official statement, research evidence has accumulated evidence that suggests the involvement of specific neurological factors in dyslexia. However, even if the origins of the condition are ultimately confirmed to be in the medical field, its manifestations continue to be educational. It is education that has to be the focus of any treatment and management.

Even if they are reassured about the word disabled some students are reluctant to accept the label dyslexia. They may experience resentment and have feelings of inadequacy over the word. Almost all students with dyslexia will experience some kind of emotional reactions to being informed that they have dyslexia. The type and degree of emotions experienced will vary according to the temperament and individual experiences of the student concerned.

Student emotional support should begin at the first assessment session. It is at this stage, when the dyslexia is first confirmed, that the counselling skills of the assessor are important. The sudden application of the labels disabled and dyslexia can be real threats to a student's self-esteem.

Some students have reported that they are concerned, when receiving appropriate concessions, that they are being given an unfair advantage compared with their peers. However, unless the support mechanisms recommended are put in place, a student who is diagnosed as being dyslexic is certainly at a disadvantage in competition with other non-dyslexic students. Students who demonstrate this kind of reaction to having their dyslexia confirmed often have emotional needs as well as practical ones. It is essential that tutors and lecturers are sensitive to these emotional needs of the dyslexic student as well as to their intellectual ones.

Self-esteem and learning

High self-esteem is a desirable personal characteristic in all walks of life. In the educational environment, it is a particularly significant factor in achievement. People with high self-esteem generally do better in their studies than those with low self-esteem. As so many

dyslexic students will manifest low self-esteem, it is important for tutors and lecturers to be aware of the effects of low self-esteem and also how they may support students with this problem. Whilst it would be unrealistic to expect lecturers to provide self-esteem enhancement programmes, it would not be unreasonable to expect them to provide a self-esteem enhancing learning environment. Before discussing the self-esteem enhancing learning environment, it is important to clarify what is meant by self-esteem and also to show how it is related to motivation.

Defining self-esteem

Like many other concepts in psychology that are also used in every-day life, self-esteem in psychology is defined in a specific way. It is best defined as the evaluation of the discrepancy between a person's self-image and their ideal self. The three concepts of self-esteem, self-image and ideal self, together make up what we refer to as the self-concept. In order to understand how the three concepts are related, each one will now be defined separately.

Self-image

This is the image we have of our mental and physical characteristics. A person's self-image is formed gradually throughout life by 'bouncing off the environment'. It is gradually developed throughout childhood so that by the time adulthood is reached most of us have a good idea of the kind of person we have become. The more experiences we have had the richer will be our self-image. As with most things in life, there will be both positive and negative aspects of our self-image. We will have compared and contrasted our abilities and our personalities with countless other people during many social contacts throughout life. We will have learned in so doing that there will be some things in which we are competent and also some things in which we are not competent.

Those who are dyslexic will have learned that they are not as proficient as many other people when it comes to the skills that are affected by their disability. The more severe the dyslexia the more negative characteristics they will attribute to themselves and so have a more negative self-image.

Ideal Self

As children develop they normally learn that the adults around them value particular kinds of behaviour such as being polite and caring for others. In other words, they are being 'socialised'. They are also learning that certain skills such as being able to read and doing well at school are also valued. In most people, this process of learning that society values particular skills and also certain kinds of behaviour, continues throughout life. For instance, most adults learn to value success in social relationships and success in their chosen employment. Under normal circumstances people learn first to aspire to these values from others but gradually begin to form their own values. The sum total of all these learning experiences is the ideal self. It becomes an ideal way of being and behaving to which we aspire.

Self-esteem

Adults will therefore have a perceived image of themselves and also an image of the kind of person they would like to become. In other words, there is always a discrepancy, under normal circumstances, between a person's self-image and their ideal self. People generally accept that there is always room for improvements and it seems to be human nature to want to better themselves in various ways. A person's self-esteem is the feelings they have regarding this discrepancy between their self-image and their ideal self. This is the concept that concerns us most in relation to academic learning. As described above, we have an idea of the kind of person we are and also the kind of person we would like to be. In most of us, there is a discrepancy between the two and this is normal. Most of us have aspirations to improve ourselves in various spheres of life. However, some of us care too much that we have not reached our ideal and this is where low self-esteem enters. In the case of those who have had literacy difficulties, the chances are that they will care very much about not being able to read and to spell, as these are highly valued skills in society. The fact that they are unable to achieve their ideal self will produce anxiety at the very least. With prolonged failure in this sphere, together with the knowledge that most other people do not have their problem, low self-esteem will soon develop.

The effects of this low self-esteem are firstly, a lack of confidence in their ability to improve and secondly, feelings of inadequacy as a person. Feelings of inadequacy with regard to their literacy skills will eventually have generalised to the whole personality. In other words, they eventually begin to feel failures as people. This is when we say they have 'low motivation;' to succeed.

The self-concept as a motivator

As described above, the self-concept is formed through experiences as we go through life. A significant phenomenon of the self-concept is that not only is it determined through experiences but that to a large degree it also determines experiences. In other words, it is a motivator. We all tend to do the kind of things that fit in with how we see ourselves. Let us imagine that we are on holiday and are looking for a social club. We find ourselves walking past a tennis club on one side of the road and a sailing club on the other side of the road. Those of us who play tennis would probably choose the tennis court while the sailors amongst us would choose to visit the sailing club.

The introvert/extravert dimension

There are many factors that contribute to differences in the way low self-esteem is manifested. The differences in expressing low self–esteem will be largely determined by basic personality characteristics.

There is one particular personality dimension, believed to be largely of genetic origin that will affect how low self-esteem will be manifested. This is the introvert/extravert dimension of personality that was described in Chapter 8. The reader may recall that the more introverted personality will prefer quieter pursuits and be happiest when working or playing by themselves or perhaps with only one or two other people. The extravert personality, in contrast, will prefer more lively pursuits and prefer the company of many people when working or playing.

This personality characteristic of introversion/extraversion can be measured along a continuum of behaviour. The introverts lie at one end of the continuum and the extraverts at the other end. The majority of people lie somewhere in the middle of the continuum and are neither extreme introverts nor extreme extraverts.

When experiencing frustration, people tend to react in terms of the above personality characteristics. For example, the low self-esteem person who is extraverted will react in an outward fashion. They are likely to try to deny their feelings of inferiority by being boastful and even arrogant. It is as if they are trying too hard to compensate for their feelings of inferiority. The more introverted, on the other hand, will react inwardly by being withdrawn and nervous in situations where they are at risk of showing their inadequacies.

It is not merely that our self-concepts tend to determine our behaviour, but also we feel more secure when behaving in ways that fit in with how we perceive ourselves. In the above example, the tennis player would probably feel ill at ease if forced to visit the sailing club and the sailor would feel the same if forced to visit the tennis club. A student with dyslexia whose self-concept comprises images of being a failure is likely to feel some degree of insecurity when engaged in tasks that demand the skills that they believe they lack. As a result they probably would try to avoid situations that demand these skills, such as writing essays or contributing to oral discussions .

Anxiety and learning

Most people will have experienced feelings of anxiety at some time in their lives. Anxiety may be mild and for some people only a fleeting moment. For others, less fortunate, it can have serious debilitating effects and require treatment. Most students will have experienced a degree of anxiety at some stage although most of them will cope. Those with dyslexia however are going to be more prone to experience anxiety and to experience it more severely as they inevitably encounter familiar failure situations.

Those who have experienced failure in school over a number of years are likely not only to have developed low self-esteem but are also likely to show anxiety reactions whenever they find themselves in these old failure situations. Whenever two things have regularly

appeared together, the future appearance of one of them will remind the person of the other one. This is the process known as conditioning. Although it could be argued that a modicum of anxiety is necessary before any learning at all will take place, too much anxiety interferes with thinking.

Cognitive Behavioural Therapy as self-help with anxiety

Before explaining the methodology of the self-help programme, it is necessary to explain some of the principles of Cognitive Behaviour Therapy. The therapy is based on the observation that our emotions are generally the result of our thinking. For example, one person sees a snake in the room and screams with fear. The next person sees the snake and smiles with interest. It was not the snake that caused these different reactions; otherwise both people would have reacted in the same way. It was the interpretation they made at the sight of the snake that caused their different reactions. It was the different thinking that occurred. The first person who reacted with fear might have thought,

'That is a dangerous creature. It can do me harm'. The second person who reacted with interest might have thought, 'This is interesting. I wonder where it came from?'. By the same token, when we say 'He made me angry' this is not strictly true. We make ourselves angry by the way in which we interpret situations and it is perfectly possible to change our thinking in order to change the emotion. So when a student feels anxious they should question their thinking at the time of the emotion.

The STAR Programme

The following is a programme devised by the author for self-help with anxiety. It is based upon the principles of Cognitive Behaviour Therapy as described above.

In Chapter 7 the suggestion was made of using a mnemonic as a memory aid. The particular mnemonic provided as an example was the word 'STAR'. This is now presented again but this time as a self-help method for a student with anxiety. It was a programme used successfully with people who were prone to panic attacks. It is suggested that students who find their anxiety disrupts their academic performance might find it beneficial to try this programme.

The Programme

The first step for the student is to remember **'STAR'.**

The letters in this word stand for

STOP, TALK, ACTION and RELAXATION.

The STAR Programme is described as follows:

S stands for STOP. This is the word that the student should use quietly to themselves immediately they begin to feel anxious. This brings thinking into their emotional experience and the effect of this is to immediately reduce the emotion.

T stands for TALK. This is what the student should do, again quietly to themselves. The talk should comprise a logical disputing of their emotion of anxiety. This means that they should ask themselves what logical reasons there are for their emotions of anxiety. The effect of this would be to reduce the emotion even further.

A stands for ACTION. This means do something physical. Whenever we feel a strong emotion we are experiencing the release of hormones, including adrenaline. By taking a walk or even just standing and jumping up and down dissipates the adrenaline.

R stands for RELAXATION exercises. These should be practised regularly in private. There are many types of exercises and there is ample literature on the subject. The student should choose the one that appeals to them most.

The success of the programme will depend on its regular practice. It will become more effective the more it is used.

The aim of the STAR Programme is to help students who may be experiencing mild anxiety and which might become disruptive if not dealt with. The procedure outlined is a ready-made method of self-help for that type of student. Where the anxiety is severe it would be advisable for the student to discuss this approach to reducing anxiety with a counsellor or a professional familiar with Cognitive Behaviour Therapy. They would be able to answer any questions the student may have on this programme or offer alternative approaches for treating anxiety.

A self-esteem enhancing learning environment

In a small-scale study conducted by the author several years ago a sample of adults who had literacy difficulties received tuition using a specific self-esteem enhancement approach (Lawrence, 2000). Their tutors had been briefed earlier in how to provide this self-esteem enhancement. The literacy skills of this group were matched with another group that did not receive the self-esteem enhancement experiences. After a 10 week teaching period the self-esteem enhancement group showed significantly higher rises in reading, spelling attainments and self-esteem, compared with the group that did not receive the extra treatment.

The value of teaching within a self-esteem enhancing environment was illustrated with this small study. In essence this means the adoption of a positive, encouraging and accepting attitude towards the student with dyslexia. In these days of larger than usual lecturing groups, it is not always possible for lecturers to have the opportunity to make a personal relationship with their students. The following notes should be helpful for those who do have opportunity to meet their students on a personal level.

Lecturers and tutors can approach their teaching in two different ways. They can teach in a way that is impersonal and without making a relationship with their students. On the other hand, they can teach in the opposite fashion, in a more personal way that allows for the establishing of relationships with their students. There is research evidence to show that the latter way is more conducive to enhancing students' self-esteem. Lecturers and tutors are in a unique position to affect their student's self-esteem by organising this self-esteem enhancing environment.

The following four principles are listed for lecturers and tutors to help them establish this kind of environment.

1. The student needs to know that their lecture/tutor understands how their disability affects their progress and is prepared to organise their teaching accordingly.

The lecturer/tutor should aim at establishing with the student the kind of relationship within which the student feels accepted, valued and understood. This does not mean showing sympathy for their disability. It is not unnatural to want to show sympathy towards a person once you are made aware of the fact that they have a disability. However, this is not always a wise move, especially if the aim is to enhance self-esteem. Most people with a disability, and especially those who have been diagnosed as being dyslexic, require understanding rather than sympathy. To be openly sympathetic to a person with dyslexia in the context of academic learning is easily perceived as being patronising. While a patronising attitude may not

do any long-term harm it will interfere with the relationship and prevent the lecturer from establishing a self-esteem enhancing one.

2. The student needs to receive positive reinforcement for effort.

Lecturers and tutors need to be alert for opportunity to praise students for their efforts even if their performance may not always warrant praise. If self-esteem is particularly low, students are likely at first to reject praise. This may seem strange but the fact is that the self-image is resistant to change; it requires many positive experiences to change it. The lecturer should be prepared for this and persist with praising where praise is due.

3. The lecturer/tutor needs to communicate to the student that they are optimistic regarding the student's potential to make progress

There is a well-known phenomenon in psychology known as the 'expectancy effect'. The expectancy effect relates to the lecturer/tutor attitude regarding their belief in the student's potential to succeed. When a trusting relationship has been established between teacher and student the student will tend to behave according to the expectancies of the teacher. The way this happens is not altogether clear but it seems that the teacher's expectancies are communicated unconsciously through body language as well as through what is said to the student. It means that lecturers need to develop an optimistic attitude at all times with regard to their belief in their student's academic potential.

4. Being aware of the skills of active listening and empathy

The skills of active listening and the ability to relate with empathy to people are probably the most important skills in a counsellor's repertoire. While it is not suggested that lecturers and tutors should set out to be counsellors it is useful for them to be aware of these skills when talking to students. Active listening and empathy mean first listening to the student's words, trying to understand the feelings behind the words and then being able to communicate this back to the student. The following are examples illustrate firstly a scene that is NOT recommended and the second scene illustrates the preferred technique.

***Scene 1** (without active listening and empathy)*

Student	(With anxiety.) I think I am going to be too busy with other work to be able to submit the assignment you have set me in the required time.
Lecturer	(With irritation.) I must point out that you have been late in the past with assignments so I ask you to do you best to finish it in time. It is essential that the assignment be submitted within the required time. I can accept no excuses for a late submission.
Student	(Quietly to himself.) These lecturers never understand the pressure I am under. I think I might leave this course.
Lecturer	What did you say?
Student	Oh! Nothing really.
Lecturer	Well if that is all; close the door after you.

***Scene 2.** (With active listening and empathy.)*

Student	(With anxiety.) I think I am going to be too busy with other work to be able to submit the assignment you have set me in the required time.
Lecturer	(With active listening and empathy.) You sound to be anxious about being able to finish it. I remember you have been late in the past with other assignments. Is there a problem I can help with?

Student (Relieved but apprehensive.) Well, I have been told that I am dyslexic. I don't really want special treatment but I do find that I am slower than the others.

Lecturer I was not aware of the dyslexia. I would like to see a copy of the dyslexia report if that is OK with you. I feel sure I can help you.

Student (Brightening up.) Sure. I have it right here. (offers it)

Lecturer (Reading report.) I'm glad you told me about this. It explains why you have been late in the past with assignments. I am going to arrange for you to have a time extension for this one. Is there anything else I can help you with?

Student (Much happier now.) No, I don't think so. But thanks a lot for listening. It will make a big difference to have extra time. Thank you.

Lecturer (Smiling.) That's OK you are entitled to concessions. After all the dyslexia is not your fault is it? See you at the next lecture.

Comment

In the first scene without active listening or empathy the student was left feeling discouraged and was considering giving up studies. In the second scene with active listening and empathy the student was left feeling supported and encouraged.

Professional counselling

In rare cases, a student's emotional needs may be more obviously debilitating and may even be manifested through disruptive behaviour. In such cases the lecturer will have to refer the student to a formal counselling service. The agreement of the student for this step must always be obtained beforehand. The lecturer's own educational institution may have their own Student Counselling Service, in which case there is no problem of where to refer the student. If there is no official counselling service within the lecturer's institution, a referral to an outside counsellor would have to be made. There are many practising counsellors but it is important that the referral is made to one who is a member of the British Association of Counsellors and

Psychotherapists (BACP). Some counsellors may require a referral from a General Practitioner.

Self-help for low self-esteem

The step of agreeing to accept counselling is not an easy step to take for some students. In fact, many students will refuse the suggestion as they perceive it to be a further confirmation of their feelings of inadequacy. In these cases, if time allows it, the lecturer might like to introduce to the student a self-help programme designed specifically to enhance self-esteem. The following self-esteem programme has been devised by the author and found to be successful for many students with low self-esteem.

10-day self-esteem enhancement programme

Day 1 Make a list of all you positive achievements no mater how small; e.g.; building a garden, winning a race, planting a tree, obtaining formal qualifications, etc.

Day 2 Make a list of all you positive characteristics; e.g.; good humoured, helpful to others, good listener, courageous, etc.

Day 3 Complete the following sentences

The thing I like best about myself is..............................

I am proud of ....

I am happy when ....

I get pleasure from ....

Day 4 Recall an event that was stressful because you said the wrong thing. Talk to yourself positively as if counselling yourself. For example, "I am not really a bad person even if what I said was wrong". Forgive yourself.

Day 5 Plan future goals. This does not have to be anything big. It could be simply putting seeds in the garden, taking a holiday, visiting a friend.

Day 6 Make decision to participate in regular exercise at least twice a week, e.g. walking for half an hour, swimming, playing tennis, etc., beginning today.

Day 7 Plan to be kind to your body by eating and drinking in moderation.

Day 8 Decide to put at least 10 minutes per day aside for complete relaxation with eyes closed.

Day 9 Decide to greet the first person you meet that day with a smile.

Day 10 Ask yourself what you can do each week just to have fun.

The programme should be repeated until satisfaction is achieved.

An affirmation for people with dyslexia

The following affirmation could be suggested at the end of each day's activity.

Dyslexia need not be a handicap. Although I may have a weakness in one area I have strengths in other areas.

For further information and details on enhancing self-esteem for students and for teachers refer to Teaching with Confidence; a Guide to Enhancing Teacher Self-Esteem (Lawrence, 1999) and Building Self-esteem With Adult Learners (Lawrence, 2000).

Summary

The student's need for emotional support has been discussed in this chapter. While many students in further and higher education, as well as people in society generally, will experience a degree of anxiety at some stage, those with dyslexia have been seen to be at particular risk. Students who have dyslexia are often anxious about the label *dyslexia* as well as the label *disabled* and will require reassurance as these labels can be threats to their self-esteem. This reassurance should begin as soon as the student is informed that they have the condition known as dyslexia.

Many students arrive at college already with low self-esteem, being conscious of previous failures in academic work. Some will be experiencing academic failure for the first time. In both cases, the research shows that these students are likely to have low self-esteem. Self-esteem was defined and its relationship to academic achievement and motivation was discussed.

Emphasis was made on the importance of the lecturer and tutor teaching within a self-esteem enhancing learning framework. The four principles involved in the establishment of this kind of teaching environment were outlined.

Not only will some of these students experience low self-esteem but some will also have a degree of anxiety that can cause disruptive thinking and so exacerbate their failures. Methods of supporting students with anxiety that can be provided by the lecturer or tutor and also by a self-help programme have been outlined. The severity of anxiety reactions will vary from mild to severe. Those students whose anxiety is mild may well be able to help themselves cope through the self-help programme that has been outlined. Those with more severe anxiety reactions will require skilled help from a professional counsellor. A student self-help programme for self-esteem enhancement was also outlined.

Chapter 10
Do students with dyslexia need preparation for life after formal education?

Introduction

It is not unusual for students, as well as staff members, to register concern over what will happen to dyslexic students when they leave the relatively sheltered college environment.

Adult students with dyslexia would usually have had time to come to terms with their disability during the course of their studies. As described in the previous two chapters, most students would have received appropriate support from various sources and eventually the dyslexia would no longer have been a major problem to them in their studies. Once they have left the academic environment, however, the situation changes and old insecurities regarding their dyslexia can so easily resurface. Without further support and understanding they can often experience problems again in the work place, in social situations and in tasks encountered during everyday living. Those tutors and lecturers who are close to their students often find they are being approached by their students for advice after leaving their studies. The main areas of their concern are discussed in this chapter.

There are numerous situations in everyday life when the person with dyslexia is likely to be disadvantaged. One example would be the premium that is placed on speed in modern society. Any activity that demands speed is potentially stressful for somebody with dyslexia. The chapter discusses some of the situations in which people with dyslexia might be expected to encounter difficulties once they have left college.

The chapter begins with discussing society's attitudes towards dyslexia. This is followed by a discussion of the problems people with dyslexia are likely to experience in the work place. Suggestions are made for careers that may be particularly suited to those with dyslexia as well as those careers that perhaps are not so suitable. The various myths in society that have sprung up over the years regarding dyslexia are also mentioned.

The problems that can arise when a person with dyslexia enters into a close relationship are discussed and also the special problems faced when the person with dyslexia is a parent.

Reference is also made to adult education classes attended by many adults keen to further their education. During these classes some adults are identified for the first time as being dyslexic. Most of these adults went to school before the current methods of identifying dyslexia were developed. Classes in adult education often comprise a number of people who are subsequently diagnosed as having dyslexia.

Finally, the chapter examines the use of the word dyslexia. There are still some people, even professionals working with learning difficulties, who are reluctant to use the term. The advantages and disadvantages of using the label of dyslexia are discussed.

The chapter concludes with words of encouragement for people with dyslexia, advocating the adoption of a positive attitude towards it.

Society's attitudes towards dyslexia

One of the problems with dyslexia is that it cannot be observed directly. In the case of most physical disabilities, the actual condition can be seen. Dyslexia, on the other hand, cannot be observed directly like a physical disability. Consequently, as people do not easily see evidence of the dyslexia, there is a natural reluctance to make allowances for it. One example of this would be those with a weakness in working memory who forget instructions. This often causes other people to become irritated and impatient. Even where other people may have been informed of their dyslexia, it is not easy for them to appreciate the everyday difficulties that a weakness in working memory can present.

A parallel with this lack of appreciation of the nature of dyslexia would be people who have a hearing problem. A hearing loss is an example of another hidden difficulty. It is reported that that people with a hearing loss often encounter a similar lack of understanding. The person with dyslexia should be prepared for a similar irritated response at times from some unthinking people. Sadly, it seems to be a natural phenomenon of human nature to be suspicious of others who are different.

Ignorance in society generally regarding the meaning of dyslexia is perhaps the greatest challenge facing those with dyslexia. Even if it is known that a person been diagnosed as being dyslexic it is rare, outside the educational environment, for people to actually understand what it means. Some people even seem to equate dyslexia with a lack of intelligence.

The obvious solution to these negative attitudes so often encountered in society would be for more education regarding dyslexia, including its definition and the ways in which it is manifested.

Coping with a public display of dyslexia

Any public display of a personal weakness is potentially stressful and a threat to the self-esteem of most of us. In modern life there are many situations where people are expected to perform in public so most of us have to face that kind of challenge at some time or other. The challenge is exacerbated for the person with dyslexia. One example of this is when forms have to be completed in public, as so often happens in a post office. There is an unspoken expectation from the waiting queue behind that person will complete the task quickly. This is not always possible for the person with dyslexia and it is potentially embarrassing to be seen to be slow in public.

Recent advances in technology and electronics in this digital age have placed extra demands on most people. New electronic gadgets and more complicated machines are increasingly being invented. For example, most people go through a period of insecurity when first operating a mobile phone. Again, for the person with dyslexia the challenge is exacerbated. The need to remember the precise details of how to operate these new innovations presents a particular challenge. For instance, the operation of a bank's cash point machine demands a level of dexterity and a quickness of response that most people find daunting. This can be particularly so for those with dyslexia. The act involves having first to read and to process various kinds of visual information before coordinating the visual information with the pressing appropriate buttons. In addition, all of this activity has to be completed quickly before the information disappears. Furthermore, most banks have cash points situated in a public place, so once again there is the probability of a waiting queue behind witnessing the whole operation and once again anxiety can interfere with their performance.

Having to use any kind of machine in public can be a potential threat to the person with dyslexia. The operation of car parking meters and transport ticket machines are further examples of this. Some machines can prove to be a frustrating experience in the home even though strangers are not witnessing their operation. The operating of a television set, a video recorder or the washing machine all demand skills that people with dyslexia may find difficult.

Some myths about dyslexia

Research into dyslexia and its antecedents is still in its infancy compared with most other topics in psychology. There are still many questions waiting to be answered. Inevitably therefore statements are sometimes made about dyslexia that are not yet based on scientific evidence. One example of this is the often expressed statement that people with dyslexia have special talents that will enable them to achieve greatness in their chosen field. It is true to say that there are numerous examples of people with dyslexia who have achieved great heights in their chosen fields. These include famous scientists, actors, sports people and successful heads of business. In an attempt to encourage those with dyslexia, attention is sometimes drawn in the literature to these famous people who have been dyslexic. Whilst this is a laudable aim it can also backfire and place those with dyslexia under pressure to achieve the same. In fact there is no research to date to show that people with dyslexia will achieve any higher than those without dyslexia. Very few people with dyslexia achieve fame and success to the extent of those usually held up as models. They may well do so, but if they do achieve fame the chances are that it will have been despite their dyslexia and not because of it.

Another common myth is to assert that those with dyslexia are better at spatial relationships than those without dyslexia. Accordingly it has been suggested that dyslexics will inevitably make successful architects or will achieve fame in other areas that require good spatial relationship abilities. To date there is no reliable research to indicate this. It is likely that those with dyslexia have a more developed right hemisphere in the brain and therefore their spatial abilities are likely to be superior to their language abilities. However, and most importantly, this is not to say that their spatial abilities are superior to the spatial abilities of those people without dyslexia.

Research may indeed eventually show that people with dyslexia have superior spatial abilities compared to the rest of the population. The fact remains that to date there is no research evidence to show that those with dyslexia are any better at spatial relationships than people without this condition.

Some authors have claimed that people with dyslexia are particularly suited to becoming successful engineers. Whilst this may be the case amongst a selected sample there is no research evidence to show that people with dyslexia make better engineers than those without dyslexia. The same conclusions have been made regarding the dyslexic person's ability to use computers. Once again, there is no evidence to show that these people are any better at using computers than those without dyslexia. This myth may have arisen because people with dyslexia tend, on the whole, to choose college courses of a more practical orientation.

A prevalent myth that certainly needs to be demolished is that people with dyslexia should avoid courses or work that demand literacy skills. As outlined in previous chapters, a student with identified dyslexia is entitled to receive appropriate support as well as various concessions to enable them to engage in any college course of their choosing. *The Disability Discrimination Act (1995)* demands that they should not be disadvantaged in the work environment either. Accordingly, the dyslexic worker need not be disadvantaged. Their dedication to the task at hand and their determination to succeed are probably more relevant in the work situation than the dyslexia. A highly motivated and dedicated dyslexic person with a high level of intelligence would be a considerable asset in most kinds of occupations, even those that demand literacy skills. The various strategies and technological aids discussed in Chapter 7 should enable them to cope without difficulty.

Attitudes towards dyslexia in the work place

The problems faced by dyslexics when entering the work force are generally similar to those they experienced as students. For instance, their main difficulty is still in the sphere of working memory. However, as students their dyslexia was accepted and appropriate concessions were granted as a legal right. As an employee, they may meet employers who do not understand dyslexia and therefore who are not always ready to grant concessions. Ignorance of the condition means that some employers are not always sympathetic to the difficulties faced by a dyslexic employee. On a positive note, there are employers who are familiar with dyslexia and do understand the difficulties faced by the dyslexic worker. There are healthy signs in industry that governmental advice on employing people with disabilities is changing the attitudes towards dyslexia of many employers. Some employers have even been known to pay for a psychological assessment in order to help support an employee who may be showing symptoms of dyslexia.

Despite the trend to a more accepting environment in industry, people with dyslexia entering the work force are still concerned whether their disability will be accepted. As a result some prefer even to hide the fact that they are dyslexic. Many students who are about to enter the work force ask, "Do I have to declare my disability to my employer?" This is a natural enough question to ask, and an important one. The fact is that it is not a legal requirement for people to declare their dyslexia. Their dyslexia is the private concern of the person involved and each person must make up their own mind whether they wish to keep the knowledge private or to declare it to their employer. They must decide for themselves whether there would be anything to be gained by declaring it. More often than not, the decision would be made in terms of the type of work and the severity of the dyslexia, as well as the known attitude of the employer. It may advisable to enquire before commencing employment whether the particular employer has a policy or a duty of care, to those with disabilities such as dyslexia. Ultimately, whether to declare the dyslexia is going to depend on whether the specific weaknesses will be exposed by the demands of the work. Clearly, if they have severe spelling difficulties and the work regularly involves writing, it would be wise to declare their weakness as they may take longer than most to complete the work. Similarly, if the work regularly involves having to take oral instructions, it would be wise to explain that their dyslexia requires instructions to be written down or at least to be given slowly and precisely.

Judging from surveys of the incidence of dyslexia in the general population, it would not be unreasonable to expect to find many people in the work place with undiagnosed dyslexia. Whenever a person appears to be having literacy difficulties or seems to find difficulty with remembering instructions, the reason could be dyslexia. If this occurs in the work situation it would be advisable for the employee to obtain advice from a dyslexia specialist.

Strategies for coping with dyslexia in the work place

As with choosing a course of study at college, dyslexia does not necessarily have to be a bar to working in any type of employment. There are always strategies that can be used to compensate for the dyslexia. For instance, if the work demands good literacy skills and there is a problem with spelling, there are many pocket spellcheckers available and one of these could always be carried. Also, a word processor with a spell check programme is often available in many work situations.

As a result of an inefficient working memory, many people with dyslexia find that they have difficulty with organising their day. Remembering meetings and other appointments can be a problem. This can be irritating for employers and also embarrassing as well as frustrating for the person with dyslexia. Once again, there are strategies for coping with this problem. Where there is access to office support staff their timetable can be organised for them and reminders given. A pocket electronic organiser is also useful in this respect.

Jobs that demand routine office skills can be daunting to some people with dyslexia. The task of filing material in their correct order, for instance, can be particularly difficult for the person with left to right confusion. This problem can be surmounted by carefully placing a list of the alphabetical symbols alongside the filing cabinet. The task becomes easier but will still be relatively slow. With practice, however, the task becomes easier and quicker.

Verbal instructions can present problems. This is especially so if the instructions are given in an atmosphere that is not conducive to relaxation. Remembering instructions is difficult for all of us if we are made anxious. As discussed in the previous chapter, there is ample research to show that in most people anxiety will interfere with remembering. This problem is compounded where the person to whom the instructions are given also has dyslexia. Under these circumstances it is advisable to explain as quickly as possible to the person who is giving the instructions that they will need to be given precisely and slowly. The instructions may also need to be repeated while the person with dyslexia writes them down. In this way, it is possible to compensate for a weakness in working memory.

There are numerous strategies in the work place that the person with dyslexia could use to enable them to compensate for their difficulties. Many of these were discussed in Chapter 7 in connection with support in their studies.

Work to be avoided

Although, in general, dyslexia need not be a bar to any kind of employment, there are some types of work that people with severe dyslexia would probably prefer to avoid. Some work, for instance, always has a certain degree of emotional tension surrounding the work itself. This is true of work that is associated with safety issues such as air traffic control or the fire service where rapid processing of information would be necessary. People with dyslexia would be putting themselves under unnecessary pressure if they were to insist on doing that type of work. They would probably need to be given extra time and opportunity to write down instructions in these two types of employment and this could put lives at risk. So, there are some types of employment that the person with severe dyslexia might prefer to avoid.

Employment particularly suited to people with dyslexia

There is a school of thought that considers people with dyslexia to be more proficient than other people in lateral thinking, and to be more creative. Although as yet there is no reliable research to support this view, it may well be that future research will indeed show this to be the case. It is interesting to reflect that there is a firm of architects in the USA that has obtained a reputation by advertising for "dyslexics only" whenever a vacancy occurs in the firm.

People who have the financial backing and the necessary enthusiasm often form their own business. For dyslexics who are in a position to do this, it is an ideal way to cope with their dyslexia. They would then be able to employ other people to perform many of the tasks that they find difficult. There are countless examples of famous and very successful people in all walks of life who have achieved success through applying their high intelligence and without needing to write. An efficient secretary can be a boon to a person with dyslexia!

The parent with dyslexia

There is research to suggest that there is a genetic component in the condition known as dyslexia, as referred to in Chapter 1. Consequently, parents with the condition of dyslexia need to be alert for similar symptoms in their children. These days most schools will be aware that they are likely to have a number of children with dyslexia. Teachers in today's schools are generally more aware of the concept of dyslexia and are prepared for the presence of children with dyslexia. Whereas in the past, many children with dyslexia would have been overlooked, in today's schools teachers are more likely to request a formal assessment where dyslexia is suspected.

Unfortunately, there are some teachers who still do not fully understand dyslexia. This means that they are unprepared to find some of the children in their care who have the specific learning difficulties known as dyslexia. Even when a child presents with symptoms of the condition, there are teachers who would rather not ask for a psychological assessment, preferring to deal with the problem themselves. The reasons for this behaviour are complex. Some teachers find it hard to accept that they cannot help all their students make good progress. As a result they persevere, determined to find the answer to why this is so. Time passes by and the student continues to fail, much to the exasperation of the parent as well as the teacher. Under these circumstances, the parent would need to confront the problem and seek an interview with the teacher.

When parents themselves have been diagnosed with dyslexia they should explain to the teacher that their child has every chance of being dyslexic as well. If the teacher does not appear to appreciate the implications of this it may be necessary to contact the local education authority to formally request a psychological assessment.

Dyslexia and basic education classes

There are probably many older adults today who left school as dyslexic but who were never identified as being so when at school. When many older people were at school, children who failed were often categorised as being of low ability and no demands were made on them to succeed. The reason for this is likely to be that these adults were children attending school during the early days of interest in dyslexia when research was in its infancy. Knowledge of the concept was limited and there were few reliable methods of identifying dyslexia. One of the consequence of this state of affairs is that today most local education authorities have classes for adults in basic literacy skills. The problem is how to motivate those people who missed out on learning basic skills as a result of their dyslexia to attend adult education classes. Many of these people have come to accept their low level of literacy skills and find it hard accept that they are capable of improving their attainments. They have probably developed a faulty self-image and will have low self-esteem.

It is not uncommon for one member of a family to draw the attention of their parent or grandparent to the fact that adult education classes exist. This can have the desired effect of motivating the person to attend but it might also have the opposite effect of rejecting the opportunity entirely. These adult classes in basic literacy are widespread and popular. More pertinently, many of the mature students who attend are often subsequently identified and diagnosed as being dyslexic. In these instances, it is the self-esteem of these adults that requires attention just as much as their literacy skills. If those people who had missed out on their education could be attracted to attend adult classes the benefits would not only be to improve their literacy skills but also result in increased confidence in them selves and contribute toward general feelings of well-being.

Social relationships

For many people with dyslexia, their disability will only become apparent through the demands of work or through the academic environment. Outside these spheres it is normally relatively easy to avoid situations that would potentially expose their weaknesses. For instance, the person with severe dyslexia who finds word retrieval to be slow would not willingly join a debating society.

There are many social situations where a weakness in working memory could be potentially a problem. For instance, remembering names of people they have only just met and also remembering their telephone numbers. These situations however, can be dealt with by writing down the information as soon as possible after meeting them. Also, to have a weak memory is not considered in society generally to be a serious problem and can even be an endearing trait, endearing only of course to the person who does not happen to be the one with the dyslexia.

Talking on the telephone can be difficult especially if there is a weakness in auditory sequential memory. There is normally no problem when talking to friends or relatives but a stranger on the other end of the line, unaware of the dyslexia, is likely to show irritation with any delay in response or with a request to repeat what has been said. This then results in the person with the dyslexia becoming anxious and so hindering their memory even further.

Perhaps one of the biggest sources of concern to the person with dyslexia arises when they begin an intimate relationship. They wonder how the other person will react once they have discovered that they have dyslexia. Should they tell the other person about their dyslexia at the outset of their relationship? Once again, as with their employer, this is a decision for the individual concerned. Every case will be different, just as every person diagnosed with dyslexia will have varying symptoms. In most cases, it is suggested that it is the quality of the relationship that should determine when and if the other person needs to be told of their condition.

Throughout this book the growing awareness and acceptance of dyslexia has been emphasised. Despite this, there are many people in various spheres of society who just do not understand dyslexia. As a result, most people with dyslexia have experienced, at some time in their lives, rebuffs and rejection of one sort or another that may have left them with feelings of inadequacy and low self-esteem. It may also have left them with a lack of confidence in social relationships. This can be a serious impediment to any relationship if it is allowed to continue but, as discussed in the previous chapter, a systematic self-help programme that encourages the adoption of more positive attitudes can change feelings of inadequacy. Relationships can be considerably enhanced when people with dyslexia feel confident in themselves and at ease with their disability. This change in attitude will result in them being more assertive in their relationships with regard to expressing any aspects of their condition.

Disadvantages of using the label 'dyslexia'

There are many people in education who still resist the use of the word dyslexia. They claim that the use of a 'label' in connection with any kind of disability does a disservice to the person to whom it is applied. There is no doubt that the labelling of people in the field of Special Education has been a controversial topic for some years now. It is over thirty years since the government-sponsored *Warnock Report* recommended the abolition of labels in Special Education and the arguments against labelling still rage today.

Firstly, if a label is used to describe a person with a disability there is a tendency to think that different people with the same label all have exactly the same symptoms. This is usually far from the case. An example of this would be the use of the label 'deaf' to describe those with a hearing loss. The use of a single word to describe the condition implies that the symptoms are the same in everybody so labelled. Yet, it is most unlikely that no two people diagnosed as being deaf have exactly the same condition. They are likely to be different both in terms of the degree and type of their disability as well as in their personalities. This is why most people would prefer the phrase 'people with hearing difficulties' to the label 'deaf'.

This same argument has been used with dyslexia. Dyslexia is not a single entity that people either have or they do not have. Different individuals with this condition have different kinds of difficulties as well as having varying degrees of it.

Another argument that is sometimes used against the use of a label to describe a disability is that people tend to perceive the label first and the person second. It is a fact that there is a tendency in some quarters to talk of 'dyslexics', rather than people who have dyslexia. This may mean of course that the disability might come to mind first rather than the person.

A further argument against using labels to describe any kind of disability is that labels can become part of a person's self-concept and so there is always the danger of the self-fulfilling prophecy occurring. In other words, people who are labelled tend to behave in terms of their label. A person labelled as being dyslexic would recognise that officially they are considered to be disabled. They may then easily be influenced by the label to believe that they are the sort of person who is bound to have difficulty with academic work. This may mean that perhaps they will think that it is not worth making an effort. It has been known for some children, with dyslexia to assert, "I prefer to do other things like art because as I am dyslexic and cannot be expected to read and spell." They believed that they lacked ability to make progress in literacy skills and so they made very little effort to improve their attainments. These may seem to be strong arguments against using the label dyslexia. However, while there may be some disadvantages in using a label, there are distinct advantages.

Advantages of using the label 'dyslexia'

Firstly, the use of a label makes for easier communication. It seems to be a natural human phenomenon to want to classify events and concepts and then to apply labels to them. For instance, we find the label 'furniture' a useful term to describe a place where chairs, tables, beds, etc. are sold. Furniture is an umbrella term beneath which there are countless other objects. Using the label 'furniture' avoids the need to list all of the items when discussing the kind of place that sells these articles. Dyslexia is also an umbrella term beneath which there is a list of specific symptoms. So, the use of the label 'dyslexia' should present no problems just as long as it is understood that it describes a variety of symptoms. Only a further investigation can determine the precise symptoms manifested

The dangers of labelling discussed above would be minimised so long as people are aware that the term comprises a list of difficulties. Note the phrase 'as long as people are aware'. This is the heart of the matter. If people in general fully understood the concept of dyslexia the disadvantages of labelling would no longer be valid. A more useful approach to the topic therefore would be to give dyslexia more publicity so that people become more familiar with the condition and what it entails.

Many people are confused about the term dyslexia and misunderstandings are not uncommon. It seems that there is a pressing need from all of us involved in the fields of Special Education and Educational Administration to educate the public regarding the concept of dyslexia. This would be a major step in removing the lack of understanding surrounding the concept as well as being reassuring to those people with the condition and result in dyslexia being more acceptable.

Final thoughts on dyslexia

Dyslexia, over recent years, has been so well researched that the old arguments about whether the condition exists have finally been laid to rest. There is now ample research evidence to demonstrate the existence of this identifiable group in both children and adults.

In view of this increased knowledge of dyslexia, it continues to disappoint that so many people still do not fully understand dyslexia or appreciate the distress that can be caused by having this disability.

There is little doubt that there is an urgent need in society generally for more education into the topic of dyslexia to combat the widespread ignorance of the condition. One particular notion that needs to be dispelled is that dyslexia is a condition of childhood only. Although all the early research and interest in dyslexia focused on children with dyslexia there is now ample evidence to show that the problem continues into adulthood albeit sometimes in very different ways. Moreover, there is increasing evidence to show that people who are described as being dyslexic are not showing behaviour that is any different from that shown by all people at one time or another. All people at one time or another show the symptoms that we describe as being characteristic of dyslexia, at some stage of development. The difference in the person with dyslexia is that these problems tend to persist over time and are often manifested to a more severe degree of severity. There is no doubt that dyslexia is a life-long problem.

Finally, it is not dyslexia itself that will be a bar to progress but rather it is the attitude that people with dyslexia have towards their disability. It is important that those with dyslexia focus on their strengths and not dwell on their weaknesses. They should have a realistic belief in their capacity to succeed in their chosen field. One of the greatest strengths anybody can possess is self-belief. Provided they are able to maintain high self-esteem there need be no limit to achievement for those with dyslexia.

Summary

This chapter has introduced people with dyslexia to the possible problems in life generally that they may face. It has warned against the all too common ignorance of dyslexia that they may come across both in their work place, and even in some social relationships. Emphasis has been put on the strengths possessed by people with dyslexia and some prevalent myths about the condition have been outlined.

This chapter also advocated a realistic appraisal of suitable careers. Whilst no career in itself should be a bar to entry simply because a person is dyslexic, there are a minority of jobs that people with dyslexia might prefer to avoid.

The arguments encountered in the special needs area regarding the use of labels were discussed. The advantages and disadvantages of using the label dyslexia were explored in this final chapter. This chapter concluded with some final thoughts on dyslexia, advocating an increased awareness of the condition in society generally. These final thoughts also included encouragement for people with dyslexia not to regard their condition as a handicap to pursuing their goals and fulfilling their aspirations.

In conclusion, recorded below is a poem written by an adult student recently identified as having dyslexia after many years of having literacy difficulties. This poem was written shortly after her graduation from University and is further evidence of the talents shown by many students with dyslexia.

Friends

Life is a tapestry
We are but single threads
Woven into each other's consciousness
Colours fade and threads become frayed
Friends accept this without pity or ill grace

As with all things time is our mistress

We are not diminished in the eyes of those who love us

But take on a familiar and comforting hue.

Sarah Allison

Glossary

ATTENTION DEFICIT HYPERACTIVITY SYNDROME (ADHD) is a personality disorder that interferes with prolonged concentration and is manifested through restless behaviour.

BINOCULAR INSTABILITY refers to a physiological condition where eye movements tend to move from right to left.

DYSCALCULIA a difficulty with mathematics that is manifested by an inability to process symbols.

DYSLEXIA in adults is a specific learning difficulty characterised by a significant discrepancy between weaknesses in working memory and measures of reasoning ability that may be manifested through weaknesses in a variety of educational attainments as well as in everyday tasks.

DYSPRAXIA is a term used to describe people who have a weakness in motor coordination.

COGNITIVE refers to behaviour that is concerned with thinking, perceiving and processing information, including intelligent behaviour.

INTELLIGENCE refers to reasoning and problem solving ability in both verbal and nonverbal spheres.

LATERAL CONFUSION is the term given to describe people who tend to confuse left from right.

LEARNING STYLE refers to a preferred way of problem solving.

MAGNETIC RESONANCE IMAGING is a term used to describe a method of measuring the blood flow in the brain to identify areas activated by different stimuli.

MAGNOCELLS are large neurones in the brain that control sensory and motor activities and are thought to influence the synchronization of events.

NON-COGNITIVE FACTORS refers to measurable behaviour concerned with personality and emotion, such as self-esteem, locus of control and motivation.

NORMS are the test scores of a previously obtained sample of people. They are used to compare an individual's score with the average score obtained by others of the same age on that particular test

PHONEMES are the sounds associated with letters.

PHONOLOGICAL refers to the study of sounds.

SCOTOPIC SENSITIVITY is a sensitivity to certain light frequencies that causes printed material to become blurred and often appears to move.

STATISTICAL SIGNIFICANCE is a statistical term that refers to the extent to which a test score, or a discrepancy between two tests, could have arisen by chance.

STREPHOSYMBOLIA is a term used by Dr. Orton to describe children who tended to reverse letters when writing.

WORD BLINDNESS is a term introduced by Dr. James Hinshelwood to describe children had difficulties with reading and spelling but has since dropped out of usage.

WORKING MEMORY refers to the act of recalling information and then processing it, e.g. calculation of mental arithmetic sums.

Bibliography

Aaron, P.G. and Baker, C. (1991) *Reading Disabilities In College And High School.* New York: Parkton, MD.

Aarons, M. and Gittens, T. (1994) *The Handbook of Autism: A Guide For parents and Professionals.* London: Routledge.

Argyle, M. (1997). *Psychology of Interpersonal Behaviour.* London. Penguin.

Baddeley, A.D. (1986) *Working Memory.* Oxford: Clarendon Press.

Bandura, A. (1970) *Principles of Behaviour Modification.* London: Holt, Rinehart & Winston.

Bartlett, D. and Moody, S. (2000) *Dyslexia in the Workplace*. London: Whurr.

Berninger,V. and Richards, T. (2002) *Brain Literacy For Educators and Psychologists.* New York: Academic Press.

Bishop, D.V.M. and Snowling, M. (2004) Developmental dyslexia and specific language impairment: same or different? *Psychological Bulletin.*

Borsting, E. (1996) The presence of magno-cellular defects depends on the type of dyslexia. *Vision Research,* 36, pp. 1047-1053.

Bowe, J. and Parsons, L. (2003) Rethinking the Lesser Brain. *Scientific American,* August, 2003.

British Psychological Society (1999) *Dyslexia: Literacy & Psychological Assessment Working Party.* Leicester: BPS.

Brook, R. L. and Stirling, J. (2005) The cerebellar deficit hypothesis and dyslexic tendencies in a non-clinical sample, *Published online, 9 February, 2005.*

Brooks, P., Everatt, J. and Fidler, R. (2004) *Adult Reading Test.* London: Harcourt Assessment.

Bruner, J. S. (1966) *Toward a Theory of Instruction.* New York: Norton.

Bruner, J. S., Goodnow, J. Austin, G. A. (1960) *A Study Of Thinking.* New York. Wiley

Carroll, J. and Iles, J. (2006) An assessment of anxiety levels in dyslexic students. *British Journal of Educational Psychology,* Vol. 76, No.3.

Cardon, et al (1994) Quantative trait locus for reading disability on chromosome 6. *Science*, Vol. 266, pp. 276-9.

Chinn, D. J. (2001) *The Dyslexia Handbook 2000.* London: The British Dyslexia Association.

Chinn, S. and Ashcroft, R. (1997) *Mathematics for Dyslexics – A Teaching Handbook.* London: Whurr.

Cranton, P. (1992) *Working With Adult Learners.* Toronto: Wall Emerson.

Cross, K. P. (1992) *Adults As Learners.* New York: Jossey-Buss.

Demb, J. B., Boynton, G. M., Best, M., and Heegen, D. J. (1988) Psychophysical Evidence For A Magno-cellular Pathway Deficit In Dyslexia. *Vision Research,* Vol. 38, pp.1555-9.

Department for Education and Skills (2004) *A Framework for Understanding Dyslexia.* Leicester: NIACE.

Dore, W. (2006*) Dyslexia: The Miracle Cure.* London: Blake Publisher.

Evans, B. (2001) Dyslexia and Vision. London: Whurr.

Eysenck, H. J. (1977) *Psychology Is About People.* London: Harmondsworth Penguin.

Fagerheim, T., et. al. (1999) A new gene (DYX3) for Dyslexia is located on chromosome 2. *Journal of Medical Genetics,* 36 (9), 664-9.

Farmer, M., Riddick, B. and Sterling, C. (2002) *Dyslexia and Inclusion Assessment and Support in Higher Education.* London: Whurr.

Fawcett, A. and Nicholson, R. (2001) Dyslexia: the role of the cerebellum, in A.J. Fawcett (Ed) *Dyslexia: Theory and Good Practice*. London: Whurr.

Fawcett, A. and Nicholson, R. (1998) *Dyslexia Adult Screening Test.* London: Psychological Corporation.

Fisher, S. and Smith, S. (2001) Progress towards the identification of genes influencing developmental dyslexia. In A. J. Fawcett (Ed.) *Dyslexia: Theory And Good Practice*. London: Whurr.

Frederickson, N., Frith, V. and Reason, R. (1997) *Phonological Assessment Battery*. Slough: NFER.

Frith, C. and Frith, U. (1996) A biological marker for dyslexia. '*Nature,*' Vol 382, pp 19-20.

Frith, V. (1999) Paradoxes in the definition of dyslexia. *Dyslexia,* 5 (4): pp.192-214.

Galaburda, A. (1989) Ordinary and extraordinary brain development in anatomical variations and developmental dyslexia. *Annals Of Dyslexia, 39, 67-80.*

Galaburda, A. (1999) Developmental dyslexia: a multilevel syndrome. *Dyslexia: An International Journal of Research and Practice,* 5, pp. 183-91.

Gardiner, H. (1993) *Frames of Mind: The Theory of Multiple Intelligence.* New York: Basic Books.

Garzia, R. (1993) Optometric factors in reading disability. In D. M. Willows (Ed.), *Visual Processes in Reading and Reading Disabilities*. New Jersey: Lawrence Earlbaum.

Gathercole, S. E. and Baddeley, A. D. (1993) *Working Memory and Language.* Hove: Erlbaum Associates.

Geschwind, N and Behan, P (1982) Left handedness. *Proceedings of the National Academy of the U.S.A. Aug. vol.79, no.6, pp 5097-5100.*

Geschwind, N. and Galaburda, A. M. (1985) Cerebral lateralisations, biological mechanisms, associations, and pathology, *Archives of Neurology,* 42, 428-459 and 521-552.

Gillingham, A. and Stillman, B. (1936) *Remedial Work For Reading, Spelling, and Penmanship.* New York: Hackett and Wilhelms.

Gilroy, D. E. and Miles, T. R. (1996) *Dyslexia at College* (2nd Ed.). London: Routledge.

Goodwin, V. and Thomson, B. (2004) *Making Dyslexia Work For You.* London: Fulton.

Goodman, G. and Poillion, M. J. (1992) ADD: Acronym for any dysfunction or difficulty. *Journal of Special Education,* Vol. 261, pp 37-56.

Gordon, T. (1974) *Teacher Effectiveness Training.* New York: Wyden.

Gorgorenko, E. L. (2001) Developmental dyslexia: an update on genes, brains, and environments. *Journal of Child Psychology and Psychiatry,* Vol. 42, pp 91-125.

Hagvet, G. (1997) Phonological & linguistic –cognitive precursors of reading ability. *Dyslexia,* Vol. 3, No. 3.

Harris, A.J. (1979) Lateral dominance & reading disability. *Journal of Learning Disabilities,* Vol. 12, 5.

Henderson, A. (2000) *Maths for the Dyslexic: A Practical Guide.* London: David Fulton.

Herbert, M. R. *et al* (2004) Brain asymmetries in autism and developmental language disorder: a nested whole brain analysis. Oxford. *Brain,* Vol. 128.

Hornsby, B. (1984) *Overcoming Dyslexia.* London: Optima.

Hulme, C. and Snowling, M. (Eds.) (1997) *Dyslexia: Biology, Cognition, and Intervention.* London: Whurr.

Hunter-Carsh, M. (2001) *Dyslexia: A Psycho-social Perspective.* London: Whurr.

Irlen, H. (1991) *Reading by the Colors.* New York: Avery Publishing Group.Inc.

Jung, C. G. (1923) *Psychological Types.* New York: Harcourt Brace.

Katz, L. and Smith, M. (1974) Laterality and reading proficiency. *Neuropsychologia,* Vol. 17, pp. 131-139.

Kirby, A. and Drews, T. (2003) *Guide To Dyspraxia and Developmental Coordination Disorders.* London: David Fulton.

Klein, C. (1993) *Diagnosing Dyslexia.* London: Basic Skills Agency.

Kosc, L. (1974) Developmental Dyscalculia. *Journal of Learning Disabilities*, Vol. 7, pp. 164-177.

Lawrence, D (2006) *Enhancing Self-Esteem In The Classroom* (3rd ed.) London. Sage.

Lawrence, D. (2000) *Building Self-esteem With Adult Learners.* London: Sage.

Lawrence, D. (1999) *Teaching With Confidence.* London: Sage.

Lawrence, D, (2009). *Understanding Dyslexia. A guide for teachers and parents*. Maidenhead. Open University Press.

Lawrence, D. (2009). An analysis of the test results of 447 adult students assessed for dyslexia. *Bulletin: Professional Association of*

Teachers of Students With Specific Learning Difficulties. Evesham. Patoss. Nov.

Luria, A. R. (1974) Language and Brain: Towards the basic problems of neurolinguistics. *Brain And Language*, Vol. 1, pp. 1-14.

Marcel, T. and Rajon, P. (1975) Literal specialisation for recognition of words and faces. *Neuropsychologia*, Vol. 13, pp. 489-497.

Marshall, J., Caplan, D. and Holmes, J. (1975) The measure of laterality in good and poor readers. *Neuropsychologia*, Vol. 13, pp 131-139.

McLoughlin, D. (1996) Psychological assessment of dyslexic students in higher education. *Conference Proceedings (University of Huddersfield).*

McLoughlin, D., Fitzgibbon, G. and Young, V. (1994) *Adult Dyslexia, Assessment , Counselling and Training.* London: Whurr.

McLoughlin, D., Leather, C. and Stringer P. (2002) *The Adult Dyslexic: Interventions and Outcomes.* London: Whurr.

Morgan, E. and Klein, C. (2000) *The Dyslexic Adult in a non-dyslexic world.* London: Whurr.

Mortimore, T. (2003) *Dyslexia and Learning Style: A Practitioner's Handbook.* London: Whurr.

Mortimore, T. and Tilly, P. (2004) Widening opportunity for dyslexic learners: is learning style theory the answer? *Dyslexia Review, 16 (1) 15-17.*

Miles, T. and Varma, V. (Eds.) (1995) *Dyslexia and Stress.* London: Whurr.

Miles, T.R. and Miles, E. (1992) *Dyslexia and Mathematics.* London: Routledge.

Miles, T. R. (1982) *The Bangor Dyslexia Test.* Wisbech: LDA.

Mortimore, T. (2003*) Dyslexia and Learning Style: A Practitioner's Handbook.* London: Whurr.

Muter, Hulme, C. and Snowling, M. J. (1997) *Phonological Abilities Test.* London: Psychological Corporation.

Nicholson, R. *et. al.* (1999) Motor Learning difficulties and abnormal cerebellar activation in dyslexic adults. *Lancet,* Vol. 353, pp 43-7.

Nicholson, R., Fawcett, A. and Baddeley, A. (1992) *Working Memory and Dyslexia.* London: Whurr.

Orton, S. T. (1925) Word Blindness In School Children. *Archives of Neurology and Psychiatry,* Vol. 14, pp. 581–615.

Orton, S. T. (1937) *Reading, writing and speed problems in children.* New York: Norton.

Parsons, L.M. Denton, D. Egan, G. Mckinley, M. Shade, R. Lancaster, J. Fox, P. (2000) Neuro-imaging evidence implicating cerebellum: support of sensory/cognitive processes associated with thirst. *Proceedings of the National Academy of Sciences of the US.A.* Feb. Vol.5, pp. 2332-2336.

Pavlidis, G. (1990) Perspectives on Dyslexia in Neurology, *Neuropsychology and Genetics,* Vol.1. Chichester: Wiley.

Pennington, B. F. (1991) *Diagnosing Learning Disorders: A Neurological Framework.* New York: Guilford Press.

Pickering, S. J. (2001) The development of visuo-spatial working memory. *Memory,* Vol. 9, pp. 423-432.

Pumphrey, P. D. and Reason, R. (1991) *Specific Learning Difficulties: Challenges and Responses.* London: Routledge.

Raskind,W., Hsu, L., Berninger, V., Thompson, J. and Wijsman, E. (2000) Familial aggregation of phenotypic subtypes in dyslexia. *Behaviour Genetics,* 30, 385-399.

Raven, J. (1998) *Raven's Progressive Matrices.* London: Harcourt Assessments.

Reid, G. (1998) *Dyslexia: A Practitioner's Handbook.* London: Wiley.

Reid, G. (1996) Dyslexia in further and higher education. In *Dimensions of Dyslexia,* Vol 1. Edinburgh: Moray House.

Riddick, B. *et. al* (2002) *Dyslexia and Inclusion: Assessing and Supporting Students In Higher Education.* London: Whurr.

Rogers, C. R. (1967) *On Becoming A Person.* London: Constable.

Rutter, M. and Yule, W. (1975) The concept of specific reading retardation. *Journal of Child Psychology and Psychiatry,* Vol. 16, pp. 181-197.

Shalev, R. S., Manor, O., Karem, B., Ayali, M. (2001) Developmental dyscalculia is a familial learning disability. *Journal of Learning Disabilities,* Vol. 34, pp. 1-59.

Shaywitz, S. E. (1996). Dyslexia. *Scientific American,* Nov. 98-104.

Singleton, C. (1996) Dyslexia In Higher Education: Policy, Provision and Practice. Paper read to *Second International Conference in Higher Education University of Plymouth.*

Snowling, M. and Stackhouse, J. (1996) *Dyslexia, Speech and Language.* London: Whurr.

Snowling, M. (1995) Phonological processing and developmental dyslexia. *Journal of Research in Reading,* Vol. 18 (2), pp. 132-8.

Snowling, M. (2000) *Dyslexia: A Cognitive Developmental Perspective.* Oxford: Blackwell.

Spadafore G. J. (1983) *Spadafore Diagnostic Reading Test (SDRT)* California: Academic Therapy.

Springer, S. and Deutsch, G. (1998) *Right Brain, Left Brain: Perspectives from Cognitive Neuroscience.* New York: Freeman and Company.

Stanovich, K.E. (1994) Does Dyslexia Exist? *Journal of Child Psychology and Psychiatry,* Vol. 35, pp, 579-595.

Thach, W.T. (1996). On the specific role of the cerebellum in motor learning and cognition: clues from PET activation and brain lesion studies in man. *Behavioural and Brain Sciences*, Vol 19 (3), pp. 411-431.

Thompson, P. and Gilchrist, P. (Eds.) (1997) *Dyslexia: A Multidisciplinary Approach.* London: Chapman and Hall.

Thomson, M. (2001) *The Psychology of Dyslexia. A Handbook for Teachers.* London: Whurr.

Watts-Vernon (1947) *Reading Tests.* Slough: NFER.

Wilkinson, G. S. (1993) *Wide Range Achievement Tests.* Washington and Delaware: Wide Range, Inc.

Woodcock Reading Tests (1987) London: AGS Publications.

Yeo, D. (2002) *Dyslexia, Dyspraxia, and Mathematics.* .London: Whurr.

Zdzienski D (1997) *Study Scan & Quick Scan.* London: Pico Educational Systems.

APPENDIX 1
A check list for dyslexia

1. Do you confuse left and right?
2. Did you struggle to learn to read?
3. Is your handwriting often illegible?
4. Do you have a problem remembering verbal instructions?
5. Do you find it hard to take down notes in lectures?
6. Do you find it hard to do arithmetical sums in your head?
7. Do you have a problem with reading maps?
8. Is it often difficult to find the right word to say in a conversation?
9. Do you make lots of spelling mistakes?
10. Do you mispronounce words?
11. Are you late for meetings?
12. Do you forget appointments?
13. Do you miss out words when writing essays or letters?

APPENDIX 2

Sample Report

Client's Name and Address:

Date of assessment: dd/mm/yy

Date of birth: dd/mm/yy

Age at assessment: dd/mm/yy

The author of this report -

holds a current Practising Certificate, and certifies that this assessment has been conducted and the report written in accordance with in the SpLD Working Group 2005/DfES Guidelines for Assessment of SpLDs in Higher Education.

Name: **Signature:**

The author is

A qualified educational psychologist holding approved qualifications as listed above.

Current practising certificate number & issuing body:

British Psychological Society Register of Chartered Psychologists

Validation Reference Number:

SUMMARY

(Client's name) appears to be functioning at a superior level of intelligence in both the verbal sphere and in the nonverbal sphere. The results would place him/her the top 1% in verbal abilities in each of these spheres of intellectual functioning. There is evidence of a weakness in both auditory sequential memory and visual sequential memory. Speed of processing material in these modes is also slower than average. He/she has an above average level of attainment in word recognition and speed of reading. Spelling attainment is below average. The overall pattern of test results indicates the specific learning difficulty known as dyslexia.

Background information:

(Client) has a place at the University of ... to study for a degree in Computer Sciences but is concerned that he/she has always experienced literacy difficulties. He/she reports that he/she was assessed as dyslexic when at school and later at the local FE College. He/she also reports that words often become blurred after prolonged reading and tend to move.

Test conditions:

(Client) cooperated well and completed the tests without any evidence of anxiety.

ASSESSMENT:

Attainments In Literacy:

Reading

1.Wide Range Achievement Test (1993)   Standard Score: 120.

2.Spadafore Diagnostic Silent Reading Comprehension: 75%.

Spelling

Wide Range Achievement Test (1993)   Standard Score: 80.

Writing speed

Writing speed is above average. 35 words per minute.

Reading speed

Aaron and Baker Reading Speed (1994). Average.

UNDERLYING ABILITY:

(Client) completed the Wechsler Adult Intelligence Scale-III (WAIS III) and the results are presented in scaled scores * and percentile scores** as follows:

Verbal Scale	*	**	**Performance Scale**	*	**
Information	15	95	Picture completion	18	99
Digit Span	11	63	Matrix Reasoning	16	98
Vocabulary	15	95	Block design	12	75
Arithmetic	9	37	Symbol Search	10	50
Let No. Sequencing	6	9	Digit Symbol	7	16
Similarities	16	98			

*Scaled scores (0–19) rank the rank the individual's results comparison with others of the same age.

**Percentile scores (0 to 100) rank the individual's results in comparison with the general population.

These results indicate an uneven pattern of development with scores ranging from well above average to well below average. (Client) is functioning at a superior level of ability in both the nonverbal and the verbal sphere. Both general knowledge and vocabulary are also well above average. The relatively lower score obtained on the Block Design subtest suggested a possible weakness in visual memory.

Cognitive Processing: In contrast to the above results, (client) scored at a below average level of ability on subtests measuring auditory sequential memory and within the average range on subtests measuring rote memory. Visual memory and the speed of processing visual appear to be only just in the average range. There was some indication of lateral confusion causing a slight delay when selecting left from right. Phonic analysis ability was weak as reflected in the below average score in spelling.

Other relevant information: The test results may have been affected by possible scotopic sensitivity as he/she often appeared to be finding visual concentration difficult.

Recommended support

1. The weaknesses in working memory will cause (client) to be slow to process auditory information in comparison with his/her peers. I would recommend therefore that he/she be allowed to tape record lectures instead of having to take down notes.
2. I would recommend that (client) be provided with a computer with scanner to help him/her organise his/her homework essays and speed up his/her assignments in general.
3. Reading accuracy and speed of reading are above average. Spelling attainment is below average. In view of the weak spelling I would suggest that he/she take his/her essays to his/her tutor for proof reading before their submission.
4. In view of the reported visual difficulties experienced by (client) while reading, I would recommend that he/she be assessed for possible scotopic sensitivity.
5. (Client) should be granted an extra 20 minutes in every one hour of examination time to help compensate for his/her slowness to process the information.
6. In view of the identified weakness in visual memory, it would be helpful if (client's) tutors could provide him/her with appropriate handouts.
7. Provided the client has available time I would recommend remedial help for the weak spelling.

List of tests used: Wechsler Adult Intelligence Scale (III). Wide Range Achievement Tests. Spadafore Diagnostic Reading Tests. Harris Tests of Laterality. Frith and Reason Phonological Assessment Battery.

Summary of scores achieved:

The WAIS III provides further analysis by grouping the test results into four specific domains of cognitive functioning known as 'indexes'. As with the traditional I.Q. compilation, the four indexes each have a mean of 100 and a standard deviation of 15. A summary of the test results is recorded below.

1. Verbal Comprehension Index (VCI) *is the sum total of the Vocabulary, Similarities and Information scores.*

VCI = 131

This score confirms a superior level of ability in verbal comprehension. This is considered by some authors to be a measure of verbal intelligence and places (client) in the top 1% of his/her age group.

2. Perceptual Organisation Index (POI) *is the sum total of the Picture Completion, Block Design and Matrix Reasoning scores.*

POI = 135

This index indicates a superior level of perceptual organisation ability. This is considered by some authors to be a measure of nonverbal intelligence and places (client) in the top 1% of his/her age group.

3. Working Memory Index (WMI) *is the sum total of the Digit Span, Arithmetic and Letter-number sequencing scores.*

WMI = 88

This result indicates an overall below average level of ability in working memory and in auditory memory.

4. Processing Speed Index (PSI) *is the sum total of the Digit Symbol and Symbol Search scores.*

PSI =91

This result indicates an overall low-average ability in visual memory and in the speed of processing visual material.

Name: **Signature: Date:** dd/mm/yy

APPENDIX 3
Screening Check List for ADHD

1. Do you often feel compelled to move around a room?
2. Do you often fidget with your hands?
3. Do you find it hard to sit down for long without having to keep moving your limbs?
4. Do you find it hard to concentrate on an interesting TV programme?
5. Do you find it hard to listen to other people without interrupting them?
6. Do you always find it difficult to wait your turn when in a queue in a shop?
7. Do you often talk incessantly?
8. Are you easily distracted by outside events when watching TV?
9. Do you find it hard to read a book?
10. Do you find it hard to begin writing letters to friends?

If more than 5 items are rated 'YES' there would be need for further investigation

APPENDIX 4
Useful addresses for adults with dyslexia

Adult Dyslexia Organisation: 336 Brixton Road London SW9 7AA

British Dyslexia Association: 95 London Road Reading RG1 5AU

Adult Dyslexia and Skills Development Centre: 5 Tavistock Place London WC1H 9SN

APPENDIX 5
Scotopic Sensitivity Screening Questionnaire

When reading…..

1. Do you often inadvertently skip words or sentences?
2. Do you tend to lose your place?
3. Do you often misread words?
4. Do you inadvertently repeat or reread lines?
5. Do you often insert words from the line above or the line below?
6. Do you avoid reading if you can?
7. Do you dislike reading aloud?
8. Is your reading slow and choppy?
9. Do you sometimes reverse letters or words?
10. Do you prefer to read in a dim light?
11. Do words sometimes become blurred or appear to change shape?
12. Do you often need to use your finger as a marker?
13. Do your eyes often become watery or red?
14. Do you often get headaches?
15. Is it an effort to keep your eyes on the line you are reading?
16. Do you find you often need to blink?

(Reproduced and amended by permission of Karen Truscott HMS Raleigh)

APPENDIX 6

Tables showing percentage differences between Indexes amongst a sample of 447 adult students.

Table 1 Percentage discrepancies between the indexes of verbal comprehension, working memory and processing speed.	
The indexes	Percentage of discrepancy scores
Verbal Comprehension and Working Memory	95.3%
Verbal Comprehension and Processing Speed	93.0%

Table 2 Percentage discrepancies between the indexes of perceptual organisation working memory and processing speed.	
The Indexes	Percentage of discrepancy scores
Perceptual Organisation and Working Memory	97.3
Perceptual Organisation and Processing Speed	96.4%

Table 3 Percentages of students demonstrating visual discomfort, confused laterality and below average processing speed.	
Visual discomfort	34.8%
Confused laterality	60.4%
Below average processing speed	95.5%
Visual discomfort and confused laterality	95.0%

APPENDIX SEVEN

WECHSLER ADULT INTELLIGENCE SCALE STATISTICS

Standard or scaled scores

Test scores obtained on each subtest have to be adjusted for age and are known as standard or scaled scores. Standard scores are best thought of as being 'averages'. The average score for each subtest is 10. Standard scores are also used when collating the literacy test scores.

Percentile rank

Percentile scores are used in both literacy tests and in the WAIS. The percentile rank refers to the number of people who would be expected to score at and above a given percentile. A percentile score of 95 would mean that if the same test were to be given to 100 people, there would be 95 who would obtain a lower score.

Index scores

Index scores are calculated by adding together the scaled scores of specific subtests. The average range for each index is from 90 to 110.

1. The Verbal Comprehension Index (VCI)

The **VCI** considered to be a valid measure of verbal intelligence. The following subtests scores are added together to calculate this index.

□ Vocabulary – assesses the meaning of words.

□ Similarities – measures verbal reasoning ability.

□ Information – Assesses general knowledge.

2. The Perceptual Organisation Index (POI)

The **POI** is considered to be a valid measure of nonverbal intelligence. The following subtest scores are added together.

□ Picture Completion – assesses ability to concentrate and visual discrimination.

□ Block Design – measures non-verbal reasoning ability & spatial relationship ability.

□ Matrix Reasoning – measures non-verbal reasoning ability (not timed).

3. The Working Memory Index (WMI)

The **WMI** is a measure of working memory and particularly auditory sequential memory. The following subtest scores are added together.

□ Arithmetic – measures working memory through mental arithmetic.

□ Digit Span – measures auditory memory, both rote and sequential.

□ Letter-number sequencing – also measures auditory memory, rote and sequential.

4 The Processing Speed Index (PSI)

The **PSI** is a paper & pencil test measuring visual sequential memory and the speed of processing visual material. The following subtest scores are added together.

□ Digit Symbol Coding – assesses laterality & visual memory & processing speed.

□ Symbol Search – also assesses laterality, visual memory & processing speed.

www.ingramcontent.com/pod-product-compliance
Lightning Source LLC
LaVergne TN
LVHW091037080826
845145LV00002B/533
9780955676208